Louisiana

LOUISIANA BY ROAD

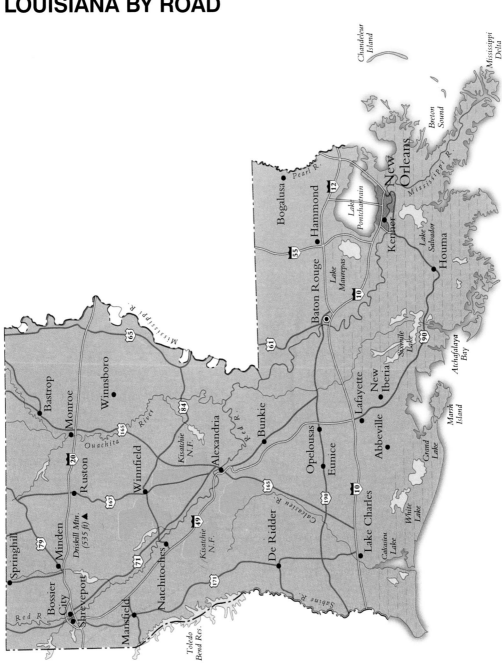

Celebrate the States

Louisiana

Suzanne LeVert

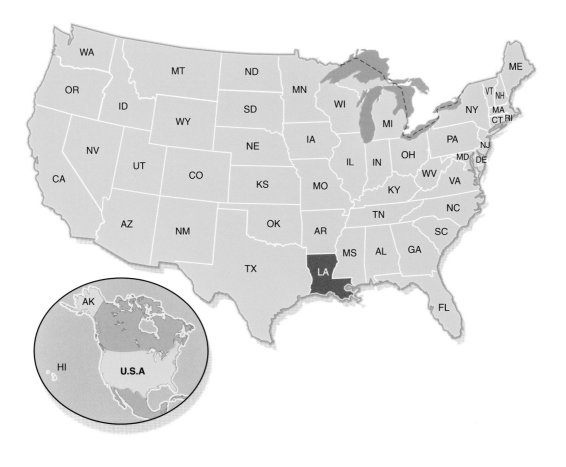

Marshall Cavendish
Benchmark
New York

Marshall Cavendish Benchmark
99 White Plains Road
Tarrytown, NY 10591-9001
www.marshallcavendish.us

All Internet sites were correct and accurate at time of printing.

Library of Congress Cataloging-in-Publication Data

LeVert, Suzanne.
Louisiana / by Suzanne LeVert.—2nd ed.
p. cm. — (Celebrate the states)
Summary: "Provides comprehensive information on the geography, history, governmental structure,
economy, cultural diversity, and landmarks of Louisiana"—Provided by publisher.
Includes bibliographical references and index.
ISBN 0-7614-2021-5
1. Louisiana—Juvenile literature. I. Title. II. Series.
F369.3.L48 2006
976.3—dc22 2005015945

Editor: Christine Florie
Editorial Director: Michelle Bisson
Art Director: Anahid Hamparian
Series Designer: Adam Mietlowski

Photo Research by Candlepants Incorporated

Cover Photo: Ken Reid/Getty Images

The photographs in this book are used by permission and through the courtesy of; *Corbis*: David
Muench, 8; Philip Gould, 10, 23, 51, 54, 57, 63, 65, 70, 77, 80, 84, 85, 86, 87, 89, 90, 95, 96, 103,
108, 109, 111, 113; Dan Guravich 11, 20; Yann Arthus-Bertrand, 13; Arthur Morris, 14; Lynda
Richardson, 18; Robert Holmes, 19; Laweson Wood, 22; Smiley N. Pool, 25; Connie Ricca, 26; Corbis,
29, 31, 32, 34, 36, 38, 39, 42, 44, 46, 79, 83, 124, 128; Bob Krist, 48; Mark E. Gibson, 62; Richard
Cummins, 66, 98; Najlah Feanny, 71; David Rae Morris, 72, 93; Joseph Sohm, 73; Jeffrey Allan Salter,
75; Alan Schein, 99; Jan Butchofsky-Houser, 101; Dave G. Houser, 107; Tim Zurowski, 115(top); Mark
Bolton, 115(lower); Brandon D. Cole, 118(top); Jerry Cooke, 126. Lynn Goldsmith, 130; Owen
Franken, 131. *Photo Researchers Inc.*: David R. Frazer, 15. *Sarah Leen/National Geographic/Getty Images*:
17. *Bridgeman Art Library/ Bibliotheque des Arts Decoratifs,Paris, France Archives Charmet French*: 28. *The
Image Works*: Bob Daemmrich: 60; James Pickerell, 100. *Index Stock*: Jeff Greenberg, 104. *SuperStock*: age
footstock, 118(lower). *Animals/Animals*: Brain K. Miller, back cover.

Printed in China
1 3 5 6 4 2

Contents

Louisiana Is . . .

. . . steeped in spicy culture

"As far as I'm concerned, New Orleans is one of three American cities that passes the Movie Test. In other words, when you're spending time in a certain city, do you feel like you've been inadvertently thrust into an actual movie? . . . As for the Big Easy, New Orleans feels like another country entirely. Is this city *really* in America?"

—ESPN.com columnist Bill Simmons

. . . tinged with scandal

"One of these days, the people of Louisiana are going to get good government . . . and they're not going to like it."

—Huey P. Long, former governor of Louisiana

. . . endowed with a strange and mysterious beauty

"It ain't Spanish, and it ain't moss."

—A swamp tour guide describing Spanish moss

"I've traveled a lot in the United States, but New Orleans is home to me now. I like it because you can go out and meet friends at cafes. There are real neighborhoods and history. It's like nowhere else in America."
—Thierry Guillaume, French-born New Orleans resident and bartender at the Uptown cafe Delachaise

. . . devastated by powerful storms

"It's only a matter of time before South Louisiana takes a direct hit from a major hurricane. Billions of dollars have been spent to protect us, but we grow more vulnerable every day."

—New Orleans *Times Picayune*, June 23, 2002, three years before Hurricane Katrina

"When can I go home?"

> —Ten-year-old evacuee from New Orleans at a
> Houston, Texas shelter, five days after the hurricane

"The levees are being mended with sand bags, and rocks, and steel bars. . . .
What should we use to mend our broken hearts?"

> —weblogger on Yahoo.com, September 27, 2005

. . . on the road to recovery

"New Orleans will always be here, in spirit and in fact. The gumbo and
the crawfish boils, the jazz and the parades, the St. Charles streetcar.
There's nowhere else but here that offers those, and there's nowhere else
I'd ever live."

> —New Orleans resident, while helping clean up
> his Uptown neighborhood

"I want the world to know what we know: we are brave, we are resilient,
and we will prevail."

> —Governor Kathleen Blano

Most of all, Louisiana is full of warm people with big dreams.

*Louisiana is unique and dynamic. It's a state with colorful politics, rich culture,
fascinating history, and, most important, dynamic and dedicated citizens.*

Chapter One

A Semiliquid Paradise

Louisiana has from its start relied on its remarkable natural resources to survive and thrive. From its intricate and powerful waterways to its underground reserves of valuable oil and natural gas, Louisiana's landscape and geological characteristics make it unique among the nation's fifty states.

While dinosaurs roamed the rest of North America some 200 million years ago, water covered much of what is today Louisiana. During the Cenozoic Era, the most recent division of geologic time, the waters receded, exposing the land. Water still covers much of the state. "The shape of the place changes minute by minute as the tides ebb and flow," says Andy Fournet, a shrimper from the bayou areas of southern Louisiana. "I'm always noticing new inlets in some places and new land where there wasn't any before."

LOUISIANA'S PLAINS

All of Louisiana lies within the fertile Gulf Coastal Plain. Three distinct regions bring variety to this low-lying land: the East Gulf Coastal Plain, the Mississippi River flood plain, and the West Gulf Coastal Plain.

"The swamps and marshes of coastal Louisiana are among the nation's most fragile and valuable wetlands," said S. Jeffries Williams of the U.S. Geological Survey.

The East Gulf Coastal Plain extends from a small portion of the state east of the Mississippi River over most of Mississippi, some of western Tennessee and Kentucky, the southwestern two-thirds of Alabama, and the western panhandle of Florida. It is the smallest ecoregion (an area of similar physical and biological characteristics) in Louisiana, covering only about 120 square miles. However, it remains one of the most vital. Later in this chapter you'll read more about the efforts to conserve that important area, especially after the devastating floods following hurricanes Katrina and Rita in 2005.

The Mississippi River flood plain is the largest ecoregion in Louisiana, covering some 12,350 square miles. It occupies parts of eight states, from southern Louisiana to southern Illinois. Within Louisiana it encompasses all lands in the Mississippi River flood plain. Flood plains are lowland areas adjacent to major rivers that flood periodically with waters that have silt and clay suspended in them. Bottomland hardwood forests and cypress swamps are the plants that dominate that region. Those forests and swamps thrive because they are able to survive extended periods of flooding.

The West Gulf Coastal Plain extends from northwestern Louisiana, southwestern Arkansas, eastern Texas, and the

Spanish moss hanging from trees and the diversity of wildlife inhabiting the waters are what make cypress swamps so beautiful.

southwestern edge of Oklahoma. In southern Louisiana, along the Gulf of Mexico, are barrier beaches. Barrier beaches are ridges of sand formed by the tides that help to protect the inner beaches from erosion. Behind the barrier beaches are marshes that extend about twenty miles north into the interior of Louisiana. To the north of the marshlands are the Louisiana prairies, characterized by gently rolling landscapes. The land gradually rises in the north, toward Arkansas, and extends as far as the Rio Grande Valley. The highest point in Louisiana is 535 feet above sea level, at Driskill Mountain. It is located about forty miles from the Arkansas state line.

Louisiana's marshes are home to wading birds such as herons, ibis, and spoonbills (above).

LAND AND WATER

Chandeleur Island

Mississippi Delta

Breton Sound

New Orleans

Pearl R.

Bogalusa

Hammond

Lake Pontchartrain

Kenner

Lake Salvador

Houma

Baton Rouge

Lake Maurepas

Mississippi R.

Mississippi R.

Atchafalaya Bay

Bastrop

Winnsboro

Monroe

New Iberia

Lafayette

Sixmile Lake

Marsh Island

River

Ouachita

Ruston

Winnfield

Alexandria

Red R.

Bunkie

Opelousas

Eunice

Abbeville

Grand Lake

Driskill Mtn. (535 ft)

Springhill

Minden

De Ridder

Lake Charles

White Lake

Natchitoches

Calcasieu Lake

Bossier City

Shreveport

Mansfield

Red R.

Calcasieu R.

Sabine R.

Toledo Bend Res.

WATER, WATER, EVERYWHERE

"Ol' Man River, that Ol' Man River . . . He just keeps rollin' along." "Ol' Man River," the song Oscar Hammerstein and Jerome Kern wrote for the musical *Show Boat*, evokes the Mississippi River's enduring power. From its source in northern Minnesota, America's most important waterway wends its way south for about 2,350 miles through Louisiana and then into the Gulf of Mexico. Along the way, it picks up millions of tons of sediment (sand and soil), which it drops when in reaches the Gulf. The land formed by this buildup is called the Mississippi Delta. The delta spreads across one-fourth of the state.

Flooding is a major problem in Louisiana. Taming the mighty Mississippi remains a concern to Louisiana, the federal government, and other states that lie along the river's banks. Since the mid-nineteenth century, the U.S. Army Corps of Engineers, assisted by state governments, has built more than two thousand miles of high embankments along the river and its

The large Mississippi River Delta region includes most of coastal Louisiana. It is a complex area of river channels, levees, bayous, swamps, marshes, and lakes.

branches. These man-made barriers, called levees, are designed to protect the land from flooding. Unfortunately, as successful as the levee system has been in protecting low-lying areas from flooding, it has had an unintended and unwanted side effect: it has also stopped the Mississippi from depositing nutritious sediment to replenish the wetlands along much of the state's coast. In addition, it appears that the levees themselves had design flaws in certain areas that led to the devastating flooding of parts of Orleans and St. Bernard parishes after hurricanes Katrina and Rita.

Another feature of Louisiana is the bayou. "A bayou is a place that seems often unable to make up its mind whether to be earth or water and so it compromises," writes the historian Harnett Kane. A geographic term unique to Louisiana, a bayou is a slow-moving body of water connected to a lake, river, or sea. The word *bayou* comes from the Choctaw word *bayuk*, meaning "small stream."

Louisiana's wetlands bring many important resources to the state. Wetlands are stretches of land in which the water lies above the surface of the ground. Unlike bayous, wetlands may be unconnected to other bodies of water. Louisiana's coastal wetlands represent nearly half the total wetlands in the United States. They support the largest fish and shellfish industry in the nation and are home to millions of native and migratory birds. Late spring and summer is an especially important time for this area. The calm waters of Louisiana's coastal wetlands and near-shore habitats begin to teem with juvenile shrimp, fish, and other sea life. Warm coastal waters and

A hungry pelican snatches a small fish from Louisiana's coastal waters.

abundant vegetation provide these organisms with the nursery grounds they need before their migration into the Gulf of Mexico.

Louisiana also has its share of impressive lakes. Lake Pontchartrain (PON-sha-trane), just north of New Orleans, sprawls over six hundred square miles. The water is brackish, which means it contains a combination of freshwater and salt water. Spanning the lake is the world's longest bridge, called the Causeway. Most of the state's freshwater lakes, including Caddo Lake, Lake Bistineau, and Catahoula Lake, are found in the northern part of the state.

Louisiana's entire southern border stretches 397 miles along the Gulf of Mexico. The ninth-largest body of water in the world, the Gulf of Mexico is one of the state's most important economic resources. Its warm waters hold abundant fish and shellfish, and oil and natural gas deposits lie deep within its seabed.

Until Hurricane Katrina destroyed portions of it, more than thirty thousand Louisianans crossed Lake Pontchartrain on the Causeway every day.

A SUBTROPICAL PARADISE

It's hot, hot, hot! When you're talking about Louisiana, you're not just talking about the spicy food or the foot-tapping jazz, you're talking about the temperature. During much of the year, Louisiana is very warm and humid. Even today, with almost every public building and private home equipped with air-conditioning, people struggle with the heat. "I think that's why things move more slowly in the South," says Johanna Weiss of Baton Rouge. "It's so sultry, no one expends more energy than necessary."

Heavy rainfall often beats down on this coastal state. On average, more than fifty-seven inches of rain fall every year. Even in the depths of winter, it rarely gets cold enough to snow. Some days in February can be almost as warm as days in August, but cold air can sweep in quickly from the north. On Christmas morning 2004, citizens of New Orleans saw snow falling steadily, bringing them the first Christmas flakes in fifty years and the first snowfall at all in fifteen years. Although most of the snow melted as soon as it hit the ground, palm trees and lawns were covered in a soft layer of white for much of the day.

Although snowstorms are extremely rare, another natural weather phenomenon is all too common. The storm Native Americans named *hurakán* is a constant threat to all the states along the Gulf. A storm becomes a hurricane when its winds reach a speed of seventy-four miles per hour. Since 1875 about forty hurricanes have ripped through the Louisiana coast, and dozens of others have missed hitting the state directly by mere miles. Two hurricanes that hit in 2005, Katrina in August and Rita in September, devastated much of southern Louisiana.

LOUISIANA WILDLIFE

Cypress trees dripping with Spanish moss; the scent of magnolias wafting in the breeze; the ungainly paddling of the brown pelican through a murky marsh; the buzzing of honeybees hovering over fragrant honeysuckle and hibiscus. The government officials who picked Louisiana's state symbols— the bald cypress tree, magnolia blossom, brown pelican, and honeybee— chose well, especially considering how much they had to choose from. Louisiana's wildlife is as unique and varied as its landscape.

CYPRESS CELEBRATION

The bald cypress is one of Louisiana's most natural treasures. In 2003 the state legislature and the state senate declared August 2003 the Louisiana Purchase Cypress Legacy Month, marking the fortieth anniversary of the designation of the bald cypress as its state tree. The Louisiana Purchase Cypress Legacy Campaign is an effort by interested citizens to designate all bald cypress trees that are certified as being more than two hundred years old with landmark status. The Legacy Campaign will then include the location of all such celebrated trees on an official state registry.

Clever raccoons can be found in Louisiana's wooded regions.

"Many people up north don't think of Louisiana as having forests," Peter Monroe of Pineville, Louisiana, remarks. "But I hunt deer in pine and oak forests up here all the time. And there are plenty of rabbits and raccoons, too." In fact, one of Louisiana's nicknames is Sportsman's Paradise, thanks to the richness of its outdoor opportunities. The Tunica Hills in the southeastern part of the state support the threatened Louisiana black bear and are the only Louisiana home for Webster's salamander and the eastern chipmunk.

Louisiana's swamps and marshlands are just as alive. In addition to harboring stands of oak and cypress trees, swamps teem with a variety of animals, birds, and fish. Human visitors to these watery habitats are sure to catch a glimpse of nutria (small rodents) paddling along and alligators sunning themselves on the shore.

In 1967 Louisiana's alligators had been hunted almost to extinction, and the federal government placed them on the endangered species list. Thanks to strict laws against hunting alligators and increased skill in wildlife management, the government took them off the list in 1987. Today, more alligators live in the Louisiana Outback than almost anywhere in the country. A 180-mile stretch of highway in southwestern Louisiana known as the Creole Nature Trail is now home to more than three thousand alligator nests.

GHOSTLY GATORS

In 1987 a fisherman boating along a bayou in Terrebonne Parish came upon an awesome and mysterious sight: a nest of white baby alligators. Although alligators have been on the planet for more than 70 million years, this was the first report of a white alligator. When scientists studied the white alligators, they discovered they were missing a certain chemical called melanin, which adds color to human and animal skin. Melanin gives alligator skin its brownish green color. Out of more than one million alligators estimated to be living in Louisiana swamps, only about five hundred are all white.

As adults, alligators have no natural predators except humans, who have hunted alligators for their hides and meat for centuries. As juveniles, however, alligators face a number of natural enemies, including turtles and herons that peck and snap at them with their sharp bills. In fact, scientists think there are so few white alligators because they make such noticeable targets for their hungry predators!

Graceful white herons and brown pelicans inhabit Louisiana's waters. During the winter they share their home with 40 percent of all the migrating birds in North America. The brown pelican is the official state bird and appears on both the state's flag and seal. It nearly became extinct in the 1960s when the use of pesticides caused the species to stop nesting along the gulf coast. In 1968 the state imported fledglings (baby brown

Brown pelican chicks (above) remain on the endangered species list. Their survival is challenged by environmental damage caused by human development and fierce weather conditions.

pelicans) in order to repopulate the area. In 1970 the federal government declared the brown pelican an endangered species. Although the state's repopulation efforts, along with new laws to protect the bird, have increased its presence, it remains on the endangered species list, except along the Atlantic coast.

Thanks to its subtropical climate, Louisiana stays in bloom throughout most of the year. The most abundant flower in Louisiana is the iris. Most irises grow in the rich bottomlands and marshes. Wild violets are almost as numerous, dotting the countryside every spring. Fragrant magnolias, camellias, orchids, and azaleas bloom over the state, from city gardens in New Orleans to wild meadows in the northwest.

THE CITY LIFE

Until the 1940s most Louisianans lived and worked on farms or in fishing villages. Today, like most other states in the nation, Louisiana is almost completely urbanized: more than two-thirds of its residents are clustered in urban areas. In fact, the state's four largest metropolitan areas—New Orleans, Baton Rouge, Shreveport, and Lafayette—are home to about one-quarter of Louisiana's population. Most Louisianans live in or close to the cities of Shreveport and Monroe in the north, or in or around New Orleans and the state capital of Baton Rouge in the south. In 2005, Baton Rouge's population nearly doubled when more than 250,000 New Orleanians evacuated after Hurricane Katrina. How many will make the capital their permanent home remains to be seen.

Each of these large cities, and many smaller ones, offers the people who visit and live in them a variety of cultural attractions, including opera and ballet companies, art and history museums, and restaurants and nightclubs.

PROTECTING THE ENVIRONMENT

Like many other states, Louisiana has paid a very high price for its economic growth. Its highest-earning industries are also among the greatest polluters in the nation, and its wetlands are being destroyed at an alarming rate.

Pollution in the Pelican State

"The old deal was a deal with the Devil—you send us the jobs and you can foul the air and the water," Representative Charles "Buddy" Roemer said in the late 1980s. Indeed, the petrochemical industries have wreaked havoc on Louisiana's land and water. In the early 1990s the state ranked first in the nation in the amount of toxic waste in its waters and third in the amount of hazardous waste it put into the ground. Only oil-rich Texas released more toxic gases into the air.

The Louisiana Department of Environmental Quality has been working hard to reverse those statistics. Since 1991 the release of toxic substances into

Louisiana's air has been reduced by about 63 percent, from more than 140 million pounds to just less than 60 million pounds. In 2004 the Environmental Protection Agency (EPA) issued a press release applauding Louisiana's efforts to clean up its air.

Nevertheless, significant challenges remain. According to the EPA, every year pollution from power plants in Louisiana shortens

Heavy industrial activity along the water's edge in New Orleans is a concern to state officials and environmentalists.

the lives of 337 Louisianans and causes nearly 50,000 lost days of work, 315 hospitalizations, and almost 8,500 asthma attacks. Air pollution from power plants contributes to almost fifty lung cancer deaths and more than five hundred heart attacks every year in Louisiana.

Shoring Up the Wetlands

In addition to offering beautiful scenery, the Louisiana wetlands provide invaluable economic and ecological resources to the state and the nation. Unfortunately, according to the state's Department of Natural Resources, the equivalent of a football field's worth of marshland is lost to open water every thirty-eight minutes, and scientists say another five hundred square miles will be lost in the next fifty years if nothing is done.

There are several reasons Louisiana is losing its wetlands at such a dramatic rate. For decades the state allowed farmers and industries of all types to dig navigation canals through marshy areas, which caused lasting damage. Global warming, most scientists agree, is causing sea levels to rise, which has also contributed to the problem. Much of the damage, however, can be tied directly to the energy industry. Scores of canals have been dug to make room for pipelines. Others, some of them one hundred feet wide, were built to accommodate barges needed to move drilling platforms into open water. In addition, the state's complex system of levees also contributes to the problem.

Even before hurricanes Katrina and Rita further ravaged Louisiana's wetlands, state officials claimed that more than $14 billion would be needed over the next thirty years to protect the coast. In late 2004 Governor Kathleen Blanco announced a plan to bring more federal money into the state to help restore the coast. She and the state legislature will request that the federal

Boat-cleared canals have destroyed the vegetation and ecosystem in Louisiana's marshes.

government share some of the more than $5 billion it charges energy companies to mine the Gulf of Mexico for oil and natural gas.

A NIGHTMARE MADE REAL

"The Big One" once was a term used by most Louisianans, particularly those who called New Orleans home, to describe a monster hurricane that would feed upon all of the city's vulnerabilities to create disaster. In addition to the damage that high winds and rain cause to areas hit by hurricanes, for instance, New Orleans has always been particularly vulnerable to flooding due to what meteorologists call "storm surges." Storm surges occur when water is pushed toward the shore by the force of winds swirling around the storm, which can increase the mean water level by fifteen feet or more. Furthermore, parts of New Orleans lie some six or more feet below sea level. Nevertheless, many Louisianans thought the "Big One" would never come, either because luck would protect the city from a direct hit or because the levee system that has long protected it would stem back the tide of disaster.

In August 2005, however, the "Big One," in the form of Hurricane Katrina, devastated New Orleans and much of the surrounding Gulf Coast area. The storm, and subsequent flooding, made true the nightmare that so long had haunted residents and meteorologists alike.

It began on Friday, August 26, 2005, when it became clear that a major catastrophic hurricane was heading toward the Gulf Coast. Many experts predicted it would hit the Florida coast, an area that had been plagued by a series of hurricanes during the prior year. By Saturday morning, however, the storm path put New Orleans in grave danger and state and city officials urged residents in the city and in the low-lying southern parishes to evacuate. Perhaps as many as 80 percent heeded the warning, but hundreds of thousands remained in their homes or found refuge in local shelters.

On Sunday night, Katrina slammed into New Orleans and its environs. Winds topped 130 miles per hour, and a drenching rain poured down on the city and the surrounding region. The wind blew out windows from high-rise hotels, tore the roofs off countless homes, and ripped centuries old live oaks from their roots. The water flooded streets and, in parts of the city, rose up to enter buildings and to float automobiles.

Despite experiencing extensive damage from the storm itself, New Orleans appeared to have dodged a deadly bullet. But the sight of relief was short-lived. On Monday, August 28, the levees that had long protected the city failed. Two breaches in these barriers allowed thousands of tons of water from Lake Pontchartrain to pour into the city, engulfing entire neighborhoods in fifteen to twenty feet of water. Hundreds if not thousands of Louisianans perished, and hundreds of thousands were left homeless. The misery experienced by its citizens and the millions of people who love New Orleans and Louisiana remains incalculable.

The flood waters that swamped New Orleans and the southern parishes ultimately will recede, but the hurricane's destructive legacy is certain to be felt for years to come as the city—and the state—works to rebuild after one of the worst natural disasters in the nation's history.

The city of New Orleans sustained catastrophic damage and flooding after Hurricane Katrina slammed into Louisiana in August 2005.

MONROE · LIVINGSTON
MARBOIS
·1803·

Chapter Two

The Rise of the Pelican State

Before Europeans arrived in the seventeenth century, about 20,000 Native Americans lived in what is now Louisiana. There were six primary groups of Indians native to the region: the Attakapa, the Caddo, the Tunica, the Natchez, the Muskogean, and the Chitimacha.

The Attakapa lived in the far southwestern region of the state. They hunted and fished to survive and did not have a very advanced culture. Soon after the Europeans arrived, the group died out except for a few isolated villages that endured until the nineteenth century.

The Caddo, a culturally advanced group, inhabited northwestern Louisiana in the Red and Sabine river valleys. They lived in small villages consisting of houses made of timber with thatched roofs. They were skilled craftspeople, creating colorful rugs, baskets, jewelry, and pottery.

To the east of the Caddo lived the Tunica, who had a highly developed economy that took them into several regions of what is the present-day

The signing of the Louisiana Purchase treaty took place on April 30, 1803. On December 10, France turned New Orleans over to the United States.

southeastern United States. In fact, they traded salt with neighboring groups of Native Americans, including the Caddo and the Natchez.

The Natchez lived in north-central Louisiana. A tribe whose culture centered around battle and warfare, the Natchez had an established war ritual that included a feasting ceremony that preceded war and, when they won a battle, a victory celebration. When they fought, they used bows, arrows, clubs, and knives. They were also known to take the scalps of their opponents.

South of the Natchez lived the Muskogean, who were related to the Choctaw of what is now Mississippi and Alabama. Living on the east bank of the Mississippi, they created clever stone implements using the gravel deposits common in the area.

Native Americans made the region of what is now Louisiana their home before European explorers found their way to the area This painting illustrates their tracking of enemies.

The Chitimacha lived in the southwestern part of the state. They were the largest of the native groups, numbering as many as four thousand when the Europeans arrived. A complex religion, highly developed crafts, and houses made of timber and thatched roofs marked their communities. Unlike their neighbors the Attakapa, the Chitimacha subsisted mainly on fish and shellfish caught from the bayous and rivers of the south.

European expansion destroyed most of the Native American civilizations in Louisiana. Diseases such as smallpox and measles brought by white settlers killed many natives, while settlers forced those who survived out of their homelands and into reservations in other parts of the country. Only one significant battle between whites and natives broke out in Louisiana. During the Natchez revolt in 1729, the tribe fought bravely but in vain against a group of European settlers. Later, in 1835, the last remaining tribe in Louisiana—the Caddo—ceded their land to the United States for $40,000.

Hernando de Soto, Spanish navigator and conquistador, explored much of the southeast during his expeditions in the sixteenth and seventeenth centuries.

THE EUROPEANS ARRIVE

Spanish explorers in search of gold and an easier sea route to Asia were probably the first Europeans to catch sight of the Louisiana shore. In 1519 Alonso Alvarez de Pineda came close to the Louisiana coast while navigating the Gulf of Mexico. About twenty-two years later Hernando de Soto arrived by a different route. He and his men trekked overland across Florida, then down the Mississippi River, almost to

THE MYSTERIOUS MOUNDS AT POVERTY POINT

An impressive seventy-foot-high earthwork shaped like a bird rises from the earth. Next to it lies a huge octagon made up of several earthen mounds. The site, called Poverty Point, is one of the largest ancient settlements in North America. It is located on a bluff overlooking the Mississippi River floodplain in northeastern Louisiana.

Between about 1800 BC and 700 BC, the people of Poverty Point established a highly developed culture and one of the most advanced commercial centers of the time. Archaeologists believe that the massive earthworks took some 5 million hours to build, a feat on the scale of the Great Pyramids of Egypt. The Poverty Point community also developed remarkable trade networks. They made stone tools from materials found in the Ohio and Tennessee river valleys. Stone tools with serrated edges are unique to the Poverty Point culture.

In 1962 the U.S. Department of the Interior designated Poverty Point a National Monument.

its mouth. Since de Soto found no gold, though, the Spanish decided not to stay.

In 1682 French explorer René-Robert Cavelier, Sieur de La Salle, sailed down the Mississippi and claimed all the surrounding land—the central third of the present-day United States—for France. He named this vast region Louisiana after King Louis XIV. For more than one hundred years France and Spain passed this territory back and forth.

The French established their first settlement in Natchitoches (NAK-i-tosh) in 1714 but found it difficult to attract settlers to this untamed and isolated part of the New World. In 1717 King Louis XV permitted an organization of traders called the Company of the West to manage the colony. Headed by John Law, the company tried several different schemes to attract settlers. Law distributed leaflets claiming that Louisiana was a "land filled with gold, silver, copper, and lead mines"—an outright lie that lured fortune seekers by the hundreds to this uncharted land. With Law's encouragement, the French government allowed prisoners and debtors to pay for their crimes by moving to the new colony.

This painting by J. N. Marchand depicts La Salle's taking possession of Lousiana.

Nevertheless, not many people came to Louisiana until 1718. That year, Jean-Baptiste Le Moyne, Sieur de Bienville, established a port city, which he called New Orleans. Surrounded by the waters of river, lake, and swamps, the French referred to New Orleans as the "Isle d'Orléans"—the Island of Orleans. Located just 110 miles upstream from the mouth of the Mississippi River, New Orleans would later become the center of the South and one of the country's most important ports.

Very quickly, the capital of the territory developed a character of its own. As years passed, European settlers brought with them fine clothing and furnishings and established elegant traditions, such as banquets and balls. New Orleans also developed a reputation as a "city of sin." Music halls, bordellos,

During the mid-1800s New Orleans became a center of commerce and trade because of its location directly on the Mississippi River.

and gambling houses opened along the riverfront, and some former prisoners and ne'er-do-wells established a network of vice.

Physically, the city could be an extremely unpleasant place. Lying five feet below sea level along the river, New Orleans swarmed with mosquitoes and other insects. Deadly yellow fever epidemics were common. The heat and humidity were extreme. Frequent flooding turned streets into seas of mud, and no sewer system existed to handle human waste.

THE SPANISH PERIOD

By 1762 France was fighting a costly war with Great Britain over control of North America. No longer able to afford to develop Louisiana, France offered the territory to Spain. For nearly forty years Spain helped Louisiana flourish and added its special flavor to its heritage. When a fire ravaged New Orleans in 1788, for instance, Spanish architects built a new city in the Spanish style, with elegant, cast-iron grillwork adorning the balconies of many buildings.

The territory's population began to boom. New arrivals from Europe joined the original French and Spanish settlers. Germans established towns and villages west of New Orleans. Scots, Irish, and British settlers arrived to settle in Louisiana's northeast. In 1764 Acadians—French settlers forced by the British to leave Canada in 1755—began to establish farms along the bayous west of New Orleans.

Slaves brought to work on Louisiana's expanding network of plantations made up the largest group of new residents. Many slaves were kidnapped and transported directly from the African regions of Guinea, the Gold Coast, and Angola. Others were taken from French colonies in the Caribbean Sea. By the beginning of the 1800s, more than 30,000 slaves lived in Louisiana, making up nearly half its population.

The large and numerous plantations in Louisiana were worked by thousands of slaves from Africa and the Caribbean.

In the meantime Louisiana played an important role in the American Revolution (1775–1783) between Great Britain and its North American colonies. Spain, a long-standing rival of Great Britain, welcomed the Revolution because it had the potential to weaken Great Britain. For almost four years Spain secretly furnished colonists with supplies and weapons.

American rebels and Spaniards often met in New Orleans because of the city's key location at the mouth of the Mississippi.

In 1800, after the defeat of the British in the American Revolution, Napoleon Bonaparte, emperor of France, pressured Spain into returning the territory to France. Once again the French flag flew over the land.

BECOMING AMERICAN

In 1803 the French needed ready cash to finance another war with Great Britain. In a landmark deal that would almost double the size of the United States, President Thomas Jefferson bought the Louisiana Territory from France for only $15 million. A year later Congress divided the territory into smaller, more manageable regions and named what would later become the state of Louisiana the Territory of Orleans.

When the people of Orleans applied for statehood in 1811, they caused a storm of protest in Congress. Some members saw Louisiana's culture as more French than American, and the territory still had a reputation for lawlessness and immorality. Despite the controversy, on April 30, 1812, Louisiana became the eighteenth state to join the Union.

Just when Louisiana became a state, Great Britain and the United States became embroiled in another military struggle over territory, the War of 1812. Two years of conflict ended when, between December 1814 and January 1815, the British tried to capture the port of New Orleans. U.S. general Andrew Jackson drew together an unusual force. In addition to the regular militia, he enlisted Choctaws and even a pirate named Jean Lafitte. On January 8, 1815, Jackson and his troops defeated the British in the Battle of New Orleans. Though the battle was fought after the official end of the war, the victory gave Louisianans a sense of pride in being American.

The British battled American forces in early 1815 in an effort to control a section of Louisiana that included New Orleans.

THE BATTLE OF NEW ORLEANS

The Treaty of Ghent, ending hostilities between Britain and the United States in the War of 1812, was signed on December 24, 1814. American forces under the command of Major General Andrew Jackson soundly defeated the British in the Battle of New Orleans some two weeks later, on January 8, 1815. Neither army had received news of the treaty at the time of the battle.

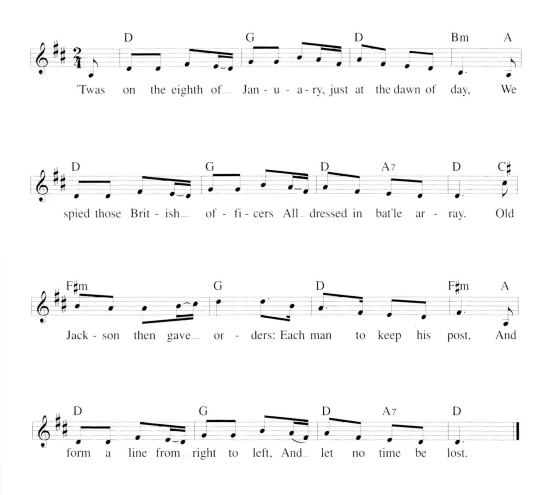

Cotton, sugar, and rice were the three most valuable crops in the world during the nineteenth century, and Louisiana's humid climate and rich soil were perfect for growing all three. More than 1,600 plantations dotted the state.

On January 10, 1812, the first steam-powered vessel puffed its way down the Ohio and Mississippi rivers all the way from Pittsburgh, Pennsylvania, to New Orleans. Goods produced in the United States near rivers now could travel more quickly and efficiently to the Gulf of Mexico and from there sail to East Coast and international ports. Louisiana could also ship its own vast quantities of cotton, sugar, and rice into America's heartland.

The Mississippi River grew in great importance as the main shipping lane in America. New Orleans was its major port.

By the mid-nineteenth century, Louisiana was no longer the isolated wilderness Hernando de Soto had discovered in 1541. New Orleans was the largest city in the South, the third-largest city in the nation, and one of the busiest ports in the world. More than 700,000 people lived in Louisiana in 1860, compared with just 80,000 when it became a state.

JEAN LAFITTE: PIRATE OR PATRIOT?

In 1806 the Territory of Orleans welcomed a new resident, one who would become a legend—the educated, charming, and dashingly handsome Jean Lafitte. Lafitte was no ordinary citizen; he was the head of a band of outlaws. With headquarters on Barataria Bay in the Gulf of Mexico, Lafitte raided ships and smuggled slaves. At the same time, however, Lafitte remained a loyal patriot, at least in his own eyes and in the eyes of many of his compatriots. When an English captain offered him money to attack New Orleans during the War of 1812, Lafitte refused. He then helped General Andrew Jackson win the Battle of New Orleans. Later, U.S. president James Madison pardoned Lafitte and his men for their acts of piracy as thanks for their service to the United States. Today, Louisianans are split in their opinions about their infamous son. Some consider Lafitte a pirate, others a patriot.

But Louisiana's prosperity came at too high a price. The issue of slavery had divided the United States. Most Republicans, who favored the abolishing of slavery, lived in the North, while most proslavery Democrats lived in the South. Tension reached a boiling point in November 1860, when confirmed antislavery candidate Abraham Lincoln was elected president of the United States.

THE CIVIL WAR IN LOUISIANA

In February 1861, shortly after Lincoln was elected president, six southern states formed a new country called the Confederate States of America. Among its first acts was to declare war on the remaining states, known as the Union. The Civil War that followed would be a devastating and bloody affair for the entire nation.

Not everyone in Louisiana wanted to go to war. Many poor whites who did not own slaves refused to fight over the issue. Businesspeople in New Orleans and Baton Rouge wanted to keep their trading partners in the north. Nevertheless, Louisiana joined the Confederacy and would fight long and hard for its losing cause.

On December 3, 1861, Union troops landed on Ship Island, located off the Mississippi coast. The war would soon come to Louisiana. Union ships led by Commodore David Farragut blocked the mouth of the Mississippi and most of the ports along the Gulf in April 1862. The blockade cut off the flow of supplies to both Confederate troops and civilians. Union control over most of Louisiana lasted until the end of the war, in 1865.

Three major Civil War battles were fought on Louisiana soil. In May 1863, 40,000 Union troops led by General Nathaniel P. Banks tried to capture the capital city of Baton Rouge by attacking its fort,

Port Hudson. Confederate troops under General Franklin Gardner fought bravely through a six-week siege but finally surrendered. The Union flag was raised over Baton Rouge.

Central and western Louisiana remained in Confederate hands, as did the southwestern Florida parishes. In April 1864 the Confederates won the bloody Battle of Mansfield. It was the last battle fought in the state and the last Confederate victory of the war. Their victory was a hollow one, however. As the Union troops withdrew, they destroyed property, crops, and livestock. Within a year General Robert E. Lee surrendered at Appomattox, and the Confederate cause was lost.

THE PAIN OF RECONSTRUCTION

The Civil War devastated Louisiana. The state's banking system had been ruined, and half its livestock had disappeared. Plantations lacked the slave labor to cultivate crops. Worst of all, some 12,000 men were killed by bullets or disease and many more were disabled.

The South's whole social structure was disrupted after its defeat. Slaves were freed and given the right to vote and hold office. The Democratic Party, once in control, now had to bow to Republican interests. In order to be admitted back into the United States, Louisiana had to allow federal officials to oversee elections. Backed by armed troops, these officials registered black voters and denied the vote to any white man who had aided the Confederacy.

Federal control over the South's internal affairs, called Reconstruction, lasted more than ten years. Although the aims of Reconstruction were admirable, the methods employed by many Republican officials were both ruthless and corrupt. Soliciting bribes, embezzling state funds, and rigging elections were common practices.

In Louisiana's new constitution, drafted in 1868, all adult males were given the right to vote, including freed slaves.

Humiliated and anxious to regain power, white Democrats of Louisiana formed secret antiblack militias, such as the White League and the Ku Klux Klan. These groups terrorized blacks and any whites who supported the Republicans. In 1874 members of the White League lynched six Republicans at Coushatta in northwest Louisiana. Two weeks later the White League overpowered the Metropolitan Police in the Battle of Liberty Place in New Orleans. A few years later Reconstruction was over, and Louisiana was readmitted to the Union.

THE BOURBON ERA

From the end of Reconstruction in 1877 until the 1920s, power remained in the hands of a small group of wealthy men known as the Bourbon Democrats. The Bourbons believed that government should not play a large role in the lives of citizens. The Bourbons also promoted the idea that white people were better than black people and should have more power and money. Because federal law gave African Americans the right to participate in the political process, the Bourbons used fear and intimidation to keep blacks from gaining power within the state. Vigilante groups like the Ku Klux Klan and the White League thrived, especially in the northern part of the state.

Under the Bourbons the majority of Louisianans sank deeper into poverty. Modern industry came more slowly to Louisiana than it did to the rest of the country. The government did not invest in improving schools, building roads, or maintaining other public services. The state remained in the grip of racism and poverty throughout the first two decades of the twentieth century.

THE LONG EMPIRE

On August 30, 1893, a boy named Huey Pierce Long Jr. was born in Winn Parish, Louisiana. As a child Long heard a lot of talk about Populism, a political movement that at that time sought to unite poor whites and poor blacks against the wealthy few who held all the power. He also grew up seeing how poor people in Louisiana lived. Schoolchildren had no books to study, and farmers couldn't get their products to market because few roads existed, and the ones that did were muddy and rutted.

Long was an extremely ambitious man. Although he dropped out of high school, he managed to get through law school at Tulane University

The popular governor Huey Long offered promise to the people of Louisiana, who then elected him to the Senate in 1930.

before turning to politics. Long ran for governor in 1924 but lost. Four years later he promised the people of Louisiana better schools and roads and said he would support poor farmers against the powerful oil, railroad, and electric corporations. The people of Louisiana, anxious to improve their lot, voted him into office.

As governor, Long accomplished many of his goals. However, he resorted to ruthless methods. He forced legislators to vote for his bills, took in and spent money freely, and ignored the law when it kept him from doing what he wanted. When challenged by a legislator who held up the state constitution, Long simply said, "I am the Constitution here." At one point during his term, the legislature removed Long from office.

At the same time, though, the state and the nation as a whole were sinking into the Great Depression. More than 15 percent of the state's population went on public relief. The people of Louisiana wanted Long in office because he made them believe things would get better. He increased funding for education and provided free textbooks for all schoolchildren. He began the construction of roads and bridges throughout the state.

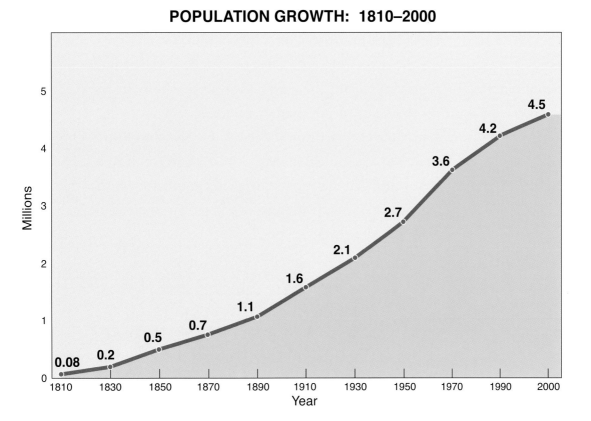

POPULATION GROWTH: 1810–2000

In 1930 Long won a seat in the U.S. Senate, although he did not give up his position as governor until 1932. He then made plans to run for president. In 1935, just as his campaign was gaining momentum, the son of one of his political enemies shot him to death in the Louisiana state capitol. Although Long's own flamboyant career ended in assassination, the state continues to feel his influence. Other members of the Long family made their mark on Louisiana, too. Huey's brother Earl served three terms as governor in the 1940s and 1950s, and stirred up almost as much controversy as Huey himself did. Huey's son Russell served in the U.S. Senate from 1948 to 1987.

INTO MODERN TIMES

In 1901 a prospector drilled Louisiana's first oil well in a small bayou town named Jennings. For the next several decades prospectors mined more and more oil, gas, and chemicals from the earth. Ever since, the petrochemical industry would form the heart of Louisiana's economy.

Louisiana did not emerge from the Great Depression until U.S. involvement in World War II snapped its economy back to life. Jobs became plentiful when the government began tapping oil, petroleum, and other industries to provide supplies. One company, the Higgins Shipyard of New Orleans, led the nation in the production of small naval craft, and the number of manufacturing jobs in Louisiana doubled between 1940 and 1950.

The social texture of Louisiana also began to change. People left their farms and fishing villages for New Orleans, Baton Rouge, and other big cities. Louisiana took its first steps toward integration. In 1960 four black children became the first in the state to go to all-white schools in New Orleans. White parents held a huge rally against integration, and violence erupted. It would be many years before race relations improved. In 1977 the people of New Orleans took a big

Before 1960 all schools in Louisiana were segregated. The 1960 school year began with the integration of African American students.

step forward by electing a black man, Ernest "Dutch" Morial, as their mayor, and today hundreds of African Americans serve in public offices across the state.

During the 1970s Louisiana experienced its biggest economic boom ever when international oil prices skyrocketed. New roads and highways were built, the education budget increased, and health care improved vastly. Then, just as suddenly, in 1983, prices on the world oil market plummeted. Louisiana's economy nearly collapsed. By 1986 it had an unemployment rate of 13 percent, the highest in the nation. The 1990s brought some improvement and by 1997, Louisiana's unemployment rate had fallen to 6.3 percent.

On September 11, 2001, Louisianans, like all Americans, were stunned and disheartened by the terrorist attacks on the nation. "I watched the [World Trade Center] towers fall and wondered what would happen to us all," recalled a lifelong resident of Baton Rouge. "I knew in my heart that we'd survive—as a country, as a state. I was humbled."

Since September 11, 2001, Louisianans have continued to work together to sustain their state's unique culture, celebrate its history, and prepare for its future—a future put into question after Hurricane Katrina hit in 2005. "I know the state will survive," claimed Matt Noble. "We always survive."

Chapter Three
A Gumbo Society

"My childhood in New Orleans was like growing up in America and not being in America," the writer Anne Rice once told a reporter. Visitors who come to Louisiana from other parts of the United States often feel the same way. The cultures they encounter here are usually very different from anything they've experienced at home. And the cultural face of Louisiana is ever evolving.

As vibrant as the people of Louisiana have proved themselves to be, they continue to face a number of challenges, including high levels of poverty and unemployment, a struggling educational system, and a soaring crime rate.

Locals like to call the state a "simmering pot of spicy gumbo." A hearty stew of vegetables, seafood, meats, and spices, gumbo is indeed an apt metaphor for Louisiana society today. In recent decades people from Latin America and Mexico have joined the Native Americans, Europeans, Africans, Caribbean islanders, and Cajuns already here, all of them adding their own special ingredients to the pot.

Louisiana's cultural mix is made up of various peoples who add to the flavor of the state.

NATIVE AMERICAN CULTURE: AN ENDURING LEGACY

The importance of Louisiana's Native American heritage becomes evident simply by looking at a map. Several of the state's parishes (political divisions) have Native American names, such as Avoyelles, Caddo, Calcasieu, Catahoula, Natchitoches, Ouachita, Tangipahoa, and Tensas. The word *bayou* derives from the Choctaw word, *bayuk*, and the names of swamps and bayous similarly come from Native American languages, including Atchafalaya, Bisinteau, Tchefuncte, and Floctaw. Even the state capital of Baton Rouge owes its name to the people who first populated the region: *Baton Rouge* is the French translation of *isti huma*, which means a "red stick," once used as a tribal boundary marker by one of the Muskogean tribes.

Although the arrival of Europeans nearly put an end to their flourishing civilizations, the Native Americans of Louisiana were crucial to the state's development, and their influence remains vital today. The Native Americans taught the French and Spanish how to fish the region's lakes, harvest its delta soil, and navigate its great rivers. Today, approximately 47,000 Native Americans call Louisiana home, making up less than 1 percent of the state's population.

The Houma of Terrebonne, Lafourche, St. Mary, Jefferson, Plaquemines, and St. Bernard parishes make up the largest group, with an estimated 15,000 members. They live in bayou towns, such as Dulac, Montegut, Pointe-aux-Chenes, and Isle de Jean Charles, and remain well known for their handcrafted dolls made of moss and for the baskets, brooms, and hats they make by weaving the leaves of palmetto trees.

About 980 people belong to the Chitimacha tribe, which has a reservation of 260 acres in south-central Louisiana, the site of their ancestral homeland. In 1971 the Department of the Interior recognized and accepted the Chitimacha constitution and bylaws. This recognition made

Native Americans of Louisiana celebrate their culture and heritage at the Caddo Adai Indian Tribe of Louisiana Powwow.

the Chitimacha the first organized tribe in Louisiana to be recognized by the federal government.

With a current membership of about 820 people, the Coushatta of Allen Parish has retained its language and continues its traditional craft of basket-making. The federal government recognized the Coushatta in June 1973, a year after the Louisiana state legislature officially acknowledged the tribe.

In Louisiana and throughout the United States, Native American people remain among the poorest of all ethnic groups. According to information published on its Web site (http://www.indianaffairs.com), the Louisiana Office of Indian Affairs was established to "empower the Louisiana American Indian people with educational opportunities to ensure gainful employment and improved quality of life through economic development." The Louisiana Indian Education Advocacy Committee (LIEAC), a group within the Office of Indian Affairs, works to support Native Americans through the school system and by working with children. Every year the LIEAC runs a camp that brings together youth from the different tribes in the state so they can learn of their differences and similarities, share cultural activities, and make new friends.

ELEGANCE AND SPICE OF OLD EUROPE

It is hard to imagine what the French and Spanish settlers thought when they first encountered the junglelike landscape and humidity of Louisiana. One early settler, Colonel James Creecy, wrote of his first exposure to the land, "The wildness and desolation will ever remain deeply engraved in my memory . . . a dreary home for alligators, mud turtles, catfish, and sea birds." Indeed, a more different environment from those of the sophisticated cities of Paris and Madrid could not exist.

ETHNIC LOUISIANA

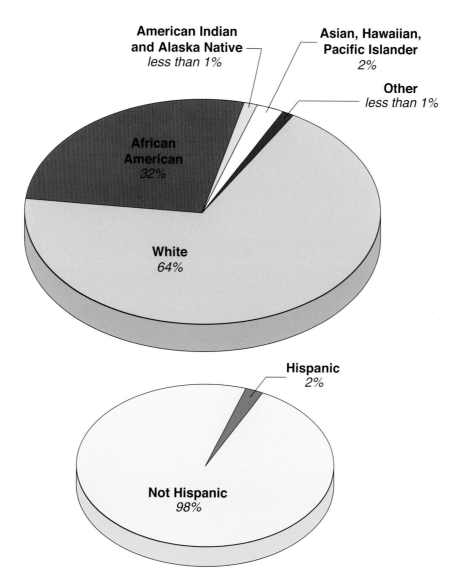

American Indian and Alaska Native
less than 1%

Asian, Hawaiian, Pacific Islander
2%

Other
less than 1%

African American
32%

White
64%

Hispanic
2%

Not Hispanic
98%

Note: A person of Cuban, Mexican, Puerto Rican, South or Central American, or other Spanish culture or origin, regardless of race, is defined here as Hispanic.

CREOLE: DEFINING A CULTURAL MIX

When it comes to Louisiana's population, the term *Creole* has at least two meanings. Direct descendants of the founding French and Spanish families can certainly call themselves Creoles, but the term has also come to denote people with both French or Spanish and African ancestry. *Webster's New World Dictionary* states the noun *Creole* comes from the Portuguese *crioulo*, which was used to denote a person native to a region. It ultimately derives from the Latin *creare*, meaning "to beget" or "to create." After the New World's discovery the word *crioulo* may have been used by Portuguese colonists to denote a New World slave of African descent. Eventually, the word was applied to all New World colonists, regardless of ethnic origin, living along the Gulf Coast, especially in Louisiana: a person of French or Spanish descent born in Latin America or on the Gulf Coast; a person descended from the original settlers of Louisiana and the French dialect as spoken by such people; and, loosely, a person with both European and African ancestors. As an adjective it means characteristic of the Creoles.

Ultimately, however, the true meaning of the word *Creole* remains unclear, with some individuals (black, white, and mixed-race) futilely claiming the right to exclusive use. As the *Encyclopedia of Southern Culture* states, perhaps the "safest" course is to say that a *Creole* is "anyone who says he is one." The Creole flag (above) represents the cultural lineage, race, and religion of the Louisiana Creoles.

Nevertheless, the early French and Spanish settlers quickly adapted to their new home. They built Catholic churches, established schools for their children, and set up a legal and political system. Many of these institutions survive today: almost every town in Louisiana is graced by a church in its center, counties are still called parishes, and the French- and Spanish-based legal system is known as the Civil Code.

The French and Spanish made several lasting contributions to Louisiana's cultural heritage. They founded the state's first symphony orchestras, opera companies, and ballet troupes. Their architects designed homes and laid out towns based on French and Spanish models that still define Louisiana's modern landscape.

Perhaps the most enduring European legacy is a social one. The traditional Creole love of food, drink, and conversation remains very much a part of the modern Louisiana lifestyle. "We all love to talk and to tell stories," admits New Orleans native Stephanie Fournier. "My ancestors came here sometime in the 1700s. The stories they passed down from one generation to the next—about everything: food, politics, you name it—could fill a lot of books."

THE LOUISIANA BLACK EXPERIENCE

Since the early 1700s, African Americans have contributed much to Louisiana's culture and society. Most of the first blacks in Louisiana were brought as slaves. The state became dependent on the slave labor that harvested its cotton, sugar, and rice crops. Life for slaves in this humid, mosquito-ridden land was brutal because of the harshness of both its climate and its slave owners. "Louisiana was considered by the slaves as a place of slaughter," wrote Jacob Stoyner, a slave who lived in North Carolina. "So those who were going [there] did not expect to see their friends again."

GUMBO: A POT OF PLENTY

There are as many different recipes for gumbo as there are Louisiana chefs. This one comes from Mary Ann Weilbaecher, who owns the Josephine Guest House in New Orleans's Garden District with her husband, Dan Fusilier.

The Gumbo Base

1 1/4 lb Creole smoked sausage (or any hot, smoked sausage), sliced 1/2 inch thick

1/2 lb lean ham, cut into 1/2 inch cubes

4 lb chicken, cut up

1/2 cup chopped green pepper

1/2 cup thinly sliced scallion tops

2 tbs minced parsley

1 tbs minced garlic

2 cups chopped onion

The Roux

2/3 cup vegetable oil

1/2 cup flour

The Liquid and the Seasonings

2 qt cold water

3 tsp salt

1 tsp black pepper

1/8 tsp cayenne pepper

1 1/4 tsp dried thyme

3 whole bay leaves

2 1/2 to 3 tbs filé (or sassafras) powder (Can be found in some supermarkets. Leave it out if you can't find it.)

Assemble the ingredients for the gumbo base, then heat the oil in a heavy 8-quart pot over high heat. (Ask an adult for help when using the stove.) Brown the chicken parts, turning them several times. Remove to a heated platter and place in a 175-degree Fahrenheit oven to keep warm.

Make the roux (paste) by gradually adding the flour to the oil in a skillet over medium-high heat, stirring constantly. Reduce the heat and cook, always stirring, until the mixture turns light brown. When the roux reaches the right color, immediately add 1/4 cup of water and all ingredients (including the chicken), except for the filé powder and the rest of the water, and mix thoroughly. Raise the heat and bring to a boil. Lower the heat and simmer the gumbo covered, for fifty minutes or so until the chicken is tender. Stir frequently. Remove the pot from the heat, then add the filé powder. Let the gumbo stand for five minutes, then serve over boiled rice.

African American communities and individuals throughout Louisiana form an integral part of the state's history, culture, and economy.

At the same time Louisiana had the largest population of free blacks in the South before the Civil War. Some arrived as free men and women from other parts of North America, Europe, the Caribbean islands, and Africa. Most were slaves whose white owners had granted them freedom. In 1856 the state supreme court ruled that "in the eyes of Louisiana law there is . . . all the difference between a free man of color and a slave that there is between a white man and a slave."

MARIE LAVEAU, VOODOO QUEEN

"Believe it or not, strange as it seems, she made a fortune selling voodoo. . . . Marie Laveau, she was a voodoo queen way down yonder in New Orleans . . ."

The song called "Marie Laveau" tells the story of one of New Orleans's most infamous and mysterious legendary figures. According to most accounts, Marie Laveau was born about 1794 and lived as a *gens de couleur libre*, or free person of color, during the nineteenth century. Although raised Roman Catholic, she was best known for practicing voodoo, a religion with roots in Africa, Haiti, Cuba, Trinidad, and Brazil. Voodoo combines a belief in one god with a belief in various kinds of spirits. Laveau acted as a mambo, or priestess. On behalf of her clients, she would invoke the spirits by drumming, dancing, and feasting, then allow a spirit to possess her. While in a trance Laveau would pass along advice or perform cures dictated by the spirit. For this wealthy members of Louisiana society paid her very well.

Marie Laveau died in 1851. According to song and lore, she was buried at midnight by the light of the moon in St. Louis Cemetery No. 1 in New Orleans. Her grave remains a popular tourist attraction, as does the Voodoo Museum in the French Quarter.

In fact, several free African Americans became wealthy and powerful enough to own their own plantations and slaves. Cyprian Richard was perhaps the richest free person of color before the Civil War. He owned two cotton plantations in Iberville Parish. Marie Therese, also known by her African name, Coincoin, had an even more fascinating biography. A child of African parents, Marie Therese was freed at the age of thirty-eight after being a white man's mistress for many years. He also gave her a small plot of land. She acquired more land and built a great plantation—so great, in fact, that she earned enough money to buy the freedom of her still-enslaved children. Her plantation, called Melrose, located near Natchitoches in central Louisiana, developed into a large community of free blacks following the Civil War.

African Americans shared their cultures with the other peoples of the state. Their languages mixed with French, Spanish, English, and Native American dialects, and so did their blood. In fact, the word *Creole*, although usually used to define the earliest French and Spanish settlers, may also be used to describe those people of mixed African American and European heritage. Blacks have certainly added spice to the gumbo pot of Louisiana culture—and quite literally at that. They contributed the use of okra (a sticky, podlike vegetable) and, along with the Native Americans, the spice sassafras (also called filé) to Louisiana cooking.

Without question, jazz remains the most enduring contribution made by blacks in Louisiana, and it is a gift given to the world. Jazz developed out of a mingling of musical traditions blacks brought with them from Africa and the Caribbean with the European music they heard in Louisiana. Louis Armstrong, Jelly Roll Morton, and Sidney Bechet are just a few of the jazz innovators who were born and bred in Louisiana. Rhythm and blues, a related musical form that uses more voices and

New Orleans is the birthplace of jazz. Here, a trombone player adds spirit to a French Quarter parade.

different tempos than jazz, also had its roots in the Louisiana black experience. Fats Domino and Professor Longhair helped develop this foot-stomping predecessor of rock 'n' roll.

According to the 2003 U.S. Census Bureau statistics, blacks make up about 32.5 percent of Louisiana's population, which is a large proportion compared with the United States as a whole, where they make up about 12.3 percent. Unfortunately, they rank among the poorest people in Louisiana: while the poverty level in the state as a whole is about 17 percent, it is approximately 43 percent in the African American community, according to figures collected by the Urban Institute in 2003. To add to this challenge, it was the African American community of New Orleans' Ninth Ward neighborhood that was hardest hit by Hurricane Katrina. Hundreds of thousands of residents remain in shelters and what will become of their former homes is unknown.

THE CAJUN EXPERIENCE

In 1764 families from Halifax, Nova Scotia, began to arrive in southern Louisiana. They joined a small community of French Canadians already living on farms along the Mississippi River, Bayou Teche, and Bayou Lafourche. These people came to Louisiana because they had nowhere else to go. They and their ancestors had lived in Acadia—the French colonies in what is today Canada. In 1713 the British took over the region during the Seven Years' War. In 1755 the British exiled any French Canadian who did not renounce the Roman Catholic religion and swear allegiance to the crown.

Once in Louisiana the Acadians developed a unique culture. Called Cajuns (a corruption of the original French pronunciation of *Acadian*), they established self-contained villages along the bayous. They lived off the land, hunting, fishing, and farming. Cajun French, still spoken today, uses words and grammar derived from a mixture of traditional French, English, Spanish, African, and Native American languages. The Cajun dialect is completely oral—no formal written dictionaries exist—yet it remains alive and vibrant in Louisiana today.

Cajuns have also added some notable culinary delights to the Louisiana pot. Perhaps more than any other group in the state, Cajuns use

The Acadian Village Museum in Lafayette recreates Cajun bayou life.

Louisiana's wildlife in their cooking. Alligator, crawfish, and turtle might never have made their way onto the Louisiana table had it not been for the Cajun flair for cooking them.

Music, too, is a part of the Cajun heritage. Using medieval French music along with traditional ballads as their base, Cajuns wrote new songs of loneliness and ill-fated love as a reaction to their brutal exile. At first they carried no instruments, but soon the fiddle became their central feature. They also used the froittoir—a washboardlike instrument—that made a "ka-chank, ka-chank" sound for rhythm. Later, they added the accordion to the mix.

Cajun music features the accordion and fiddle to achieve its rhythmic sound.

POPULATION DENSITY

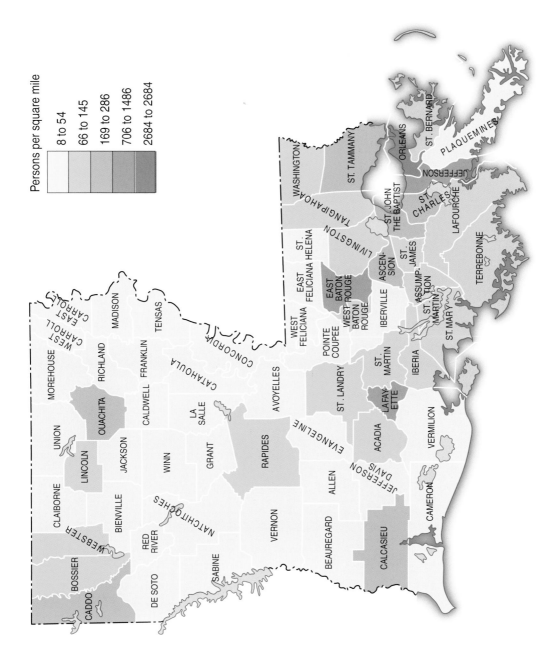

Persons per square mile

8 to 54
66 to 145
169 to 286
706 to 1486
2684 to 2684

WASHINGTON
ST. TAMMANY
ORLEANS
ST. BERNARD
PLAQUEMINES
JEFFERSON
ST. CHARLES
LAFOURCHE
TANGIPAHOA
ST. JOHN THE BAPTIST
TERREBONNE
LIVINGSTON
ST. JAMES
ASCEN- SION
ASSUMP- TION
EAST FELICIANA
ST. HELENA
EAST BATON ROUGE
WEST BATON ROUGE
IBERVILLE
ST. MARTIN
ST. MARY
WEST FELICIANA
POINTE COUPEE
ST. LANDRY
ST. MARTIN
IBERIA
CADDO
BOSSIER
WEBSTER
CLAIBORNE
UNION
MOREHOUSE
WEST CARROLL
EAST CARROLL
MADISON
RICHLAND
OUACHITA
LINCOLN
BIENVILLE
RED RIVER
DE SOTO
JACKSON
CALDWELL
FRANKLIN
TENSAS
WINN
LA SALLE
CATAHOULA
CONCORDIA
AVOYELLES
GRANT
NATCHITOCHES
SABINE
VERNON
RAPIDES
EVANGELINE
ST. LANDRY
ACADIA
LAFAY- ETTE
VERMILION
CAMERON
CALCASIEU
BEAUREGARD
ALLEN
JEFFERSON DAVIS

Cajun music has a cousin, zydeco, that was influenced by African American folk and rhythm and blues. Stanley Dural, the leader of the band Buckwheat Zydeco, describes the music this way: "You add a little blues, a little soul, a little rock 'n' roll, and a little jazz and mix it all in. Sometimes, you can hear five types of music in one song."

Although some Cajuns still make their living off the land, most have moved to the cities along with the rest of Louisiana society. Their culture, however, remains very much alive. Louisiana folklorist Barry Jean Ancelet speaks of the "uncanny adaptability" of the Cajuns: "Cajuns have always been able to chew up change, swallow the palatable parts, and spit out the rest."

FACING CHALLENGES AS A COMMUNITY

Today, Louisiana's population is among the most diverse in the nation. People from all over the world have joined the state's founding groups to give Louisiana one of the most richly textured cultures in our nation. As you've seen, though, the people of the Pelican State also face obstacles to their prosperity and growth. In the next chapter, you'll read about some of the measures the state government is taking to offer more economic and educational opportunities to its people and to improve the future of the state.

The diversity of Louisiana's population is a reflection on the state's past. Hispanics and Native Americans, as well as African Americans, Asians, and Caucasians, all call Louisiana home.

STATE OF LOUISIANA

UNION JUSTICE

CONFIDENCE

LOUISIANA

Chapter Four

Governing Louisiana

Despite its rich natural resources, stunning physical beauty, and vibrant population, Louisiana remains one of the nation's poorest states, with among the highest rates of crime, unemployment, adult illiteracy, and infant mortality. The state's government must meet the needs of its diverse citizenry and provide them with the skills and resources they need to thrive in the twenty-first century.

INSIDE GOVERNMENT

From the start Louisianans have been fussing with the makeup of their government and the laws of their state. In fact, Louisiana has had eleven different constitutions, more than any other U.S. state. The present constitution was adopted in 1974.

This constitution contains a remarkable bill of rights, one of the most progressive in the country. "No law shall discriminate against a person because of race or religious ideas, beliefs, or affiliations," the bill states. "No law shall arbitrarily, capriciously, or unreasonably discriminate against a person because of birth, age, sex, culture, physical condition, or political ideas

William C. C. Clairborne, Louisiana's first governor, was the first to use the pelican as an emblem on official state documents.

or affiliations." This addition to the state constitution shows how far Louisiana has come since its earlier constitutions, which essentially denied all but white men with property the right to vote.

"Politics in Louisiana are almost as popular as football in Indiana," remarks Dan Fournier, a native of the state. Indeed, Louisiana's politics have always been spirited and exciting, but often contentious and corrupt.

Louisiana is unique among U.S. states in that it uses a "runoff system" to elect people to state, local, and congressional offices. All candidates run in an open primary on election day in which multiple candidates from the same party may be on the ballot. If no candidate receives more than 50 percent of the vote, the two candidates with the highest votes in total compete in a runoff election approximately one month later. This runoff does not take into account party affiliation. Therefore, it is common for a Democrat to be in a runoff with a fellow Democrat or a Republican to be in a runoff with a fellow Republican. All other states use the "first past the post" system, in which each party elects a candidate during a primary, and then the candidates from different parties run against each other on election day.

Executive

The head of Louisiana's executive branch is the governor, who is elected to a four-year term. By law a Louisiana governor cannot serve more than two consecutive terms but can serve an unlimited number of terms. The governor of Louisiana has many powers and duties, including appointing judges and certain other officials, preparing the state budget, and considering proposed laws for enactment.

The office of governor is a powerful position that many ambitious, talented, and colorful people have held. Some have used their powers for good, others for personal or political gain. Henry Warmoth, who served from 1868 to 1872, was called "the shrewdest, boldest, ablest,

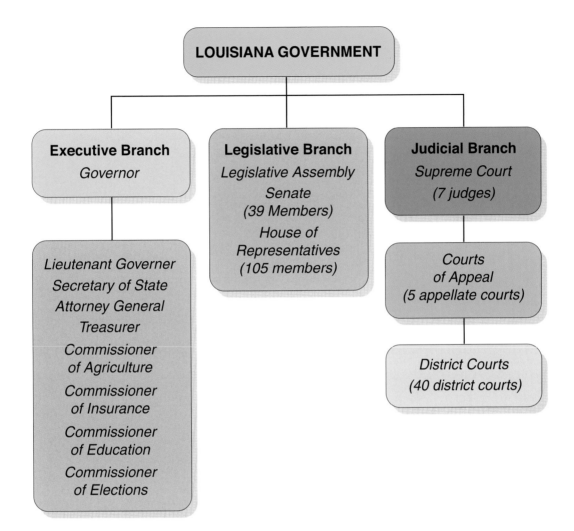

LOUISIANA GOVERNMENT

Executive Branch
Governor

Lieutenant Governer
Secretary of State
Attorney General
Treasurer
*Commissioner
of Agriculture*
*Commissioner
of Insurance*
*Commissioner
of Education*
*Commissioner
of Elections*

Legislative Branch
Legislative Assembly
*Senate
(39 Members)*
*House of
Representatives
(105 members)*

Judicial Branch
*Supreme Court
(7 judges)*

*Courts
of Appeal
(5 appellate courts)*

*District Courts
(40 district courts)*

and most conscienceless young man" by his former commanding officer, Ulysses S. Grant.

After his brother Huey's assassination, Earl Long served three nonconsecutive terms as governor (and was elected to the U.S. House of Representatives, but died before taking office), despite a great deal of controversy surrounding his personal and political life. Governor John J. McKeithen led the state through the difficult process of integration while expanding its economy during his two consecutive terms, from 1964 to 1972. McKeithen's son, Fox McKeithen has served as Louisiana's secretary of state since 1988.

Edwin W. Edwards served the most time as governor—two consecutive terms from 1972 to 1980, then again from 1984 to 1988 and from 1992 to 1996. Edwards was the state's first modern governor of Cajun heritage. He helped move Louisiana forward during its economic boom of the 1970s and then saw the state through tough times during the late 1980s and into the 1990s.

But Edwards also stirred up controversy and added to Louisiana's reputation as a politically corrupt state. A notorious gambler, Edwards once told a reporter that he kept $800,000 in ready cash for his trips to Las Vegas. In 1985 he was indicted (but not convicted) on federal racketeering charges. And still the people of Louisiana wanted him to govern. J. Bennett Johnson, an associate, once said of him, "Edwin's greatest strength and his greatest weakness is his ability to come within a millimeter of the law without breaking it." Unfortunately for Edwards, his strength finally failed him. He decided not to run for reelection in 1995, when Mike Foster won the office. In 2000 a federal jury convicted Edwards and four associates, including his son Stephen, of racketeering, extortion, and conspiracy in the awarding of casino licenses. Edwards appealed the convictions, but after his appeals failed, he entered federal prison, where he remains.

During Edwin Edwards term as governor he oversaw the creation of a new state constitution and appointed African Americans to several governmental postions.

"Vote for the Crook—It's Important."

So read a popular bumper sticker in support of Edwin Edwards during the 1991 campaign for Louisiana governor, one of the most controversial elections in the state's history. David Duke (below), a former high-ranking member of a racist organization, was pitted against former governor Edwin Edwards, a gambler once indicted for racketeering, or obtaining money through illegal activities.

The election highlighted Louisiana's traditional political divisions. Duke attracted many of the white, lower-income Baptists living primarily in the northern part of the state, while Edwards received votes from nearly all the blacks in the state and 45 percent of the whites. Most whites who voted for Edwards were Catholic, relatively wealthy, and living in the southern part of the state. In fact, were it not for the fact that 96 percent of all Louisiana's blacks—who made up 30 percent of the state's population—voted for Edwards, Louisiana might have elected a known racist to its highest office.

Edwin Edwards won the election and served his final term as governor. But by 2005 both men were serving time in federal prison, Edwards for extorting millions of dollars from businesspeople wishing to obtain state riverboat gambling licenses, and Duke for committing mail and tax fraud.

Mike Foster, a conservative Republican, followed Edwards into the governor's office and served two terms. Foster's very first action as governor stirred up a hornet's nest of controversy. He eliminated the state's affirmative-action programs designed to give African Americans and other minorities a better chance to compete in business. He claimed that these programs were no longer necessary and that employment should be based solely on merit. However, his concentration on the state's most pressing issues—a faltering school system, a struggling economy, and a high crime rate—convinced voters to elect him to a second term in 1999. He made it through his terms as governor without a major scandal, although he was fined $10,000 for violating campaign disclosure laws. Foster enacted major education reform, but he also saw the state's economy continue to falter.

In 2003 Democrats regained the governor's office with the runoff election of Lieutenant Governor Kathleen Blanco, the first woman ever to be elected governor of Louisiana. She did so by defeating the first person of Indian extraction, Republican Bobby Jindal, to run for office. The people of Louisiana voted Blanco into office for her moderate stands on most issues as well as for her promise not to raise state taxes and to advocate for sweeping governmental ethics reforms.

Governor Kathleen Blanco is the first woman to be elected to Louisiana's highest office.

Legislative

Louisiana's citizens elect members to two houses of the state legislature: 39 members to the Senate and 105 members to the House of Representatives. Both senators and representatives serve four-year terms.

These men and women work together to create and enact laws. When both the Senate and the House agree on a proposed law, called a bill, the legislature sends it to the governor. If the governor signs it, the bill becomes law. If the governor vetoes (rejects) the bill, it goes back to the legislature. If two-thirds of both houses still want the bill to become law, they can vote to override the veto.

Judicial

Louisiana's highest court is the Supreme Court, which has a chief justice and six associate justices, all elected to ten-year terms. The court system also includes five state courts of appeal and forty district courts. Louisiana's legal system is based on what is known as civil law. Civil law is based on the Napoleonic Code of France, a vestige of Louisiana's French past. Under civil law judges decide cases based on a written set of rules. They can disregard decisions made by judges about similar cases. Other states practice common law, which bases rulings on previous court decisions, also called precedents.

The state capitol building in Baton Rouge is the tallest capitol in the United States. The legislature meets here to create laws.

Mayors and Managers

Louisiana is divided into sixty-four units of local government called parishes. The term comes from the days of French and Spanish rule, when the Catholic Church called its districts parishes. Today, many parishes are governed by a body called a police jury, which acts much like a town council. New Orleans and other large cities, such as Baton Rouge, Shreveport, and Monroe, have mayors as their chief executives.

CHALLENGES AND GOALS FOR GOVERNMENT

From stemming rising crime rates that plague its cities, to improving educational opportunities and health care for all Louisianans, to protecting the state from the threat of terrorist attacks, Louisiana government officials certainly have their work cut out for them.

Crime and Punishment

In 1994 New Orleans became known as the "murder capital of the United States." Its murder rate was a shocking 966 percent higher than the national rate. For a few years after that all-time high, the city's crime rate decreased, thanks in large part to increased spending for public safety and corrections services. But starting in 2001 the crime rate began to climb. In 2003 New Orleans once again had the highest murder rate in the nation: 57 murders per 100,000 residents, more than eight times that of New York City and three times that of Chicago, Illinois.

What makes Louisiana's largest city such a violent place? Most experts agree that crime thrives in poverty-ridden places, and New Orleans is one of the poorest cities in the country. Many times crime goes hand in hand with drugs—not only are possessing and selling drugs crimes themselves, but that lifestyle can often trigger a user or seller to commit other offenses, such as theft, burglary, and murder. According to statistics published by the Office of National Drug Control Policy, more than 78 percent of adult male and nearly 60 percent of adult female arrestees in New Orleans tested positive for cocaine, heroin, marijuana, methamphetamine, or PCP (sometimes called angel dust) at the time of their arrest in 2003. In a series of newspaper articles chronicling New Orleans's struggle with crime, the *Times-Picayune* pointed out another startling statistic: of the 274 people murdered in the city in 2003, nearly all had criminal records, and 104 of them were killed within three months of their last arrest.

The latest statistics available show that the murder rate in New Orleans declined by about 4 percent in 2004, while rates of other crimes remained steady. Local and federal law enforcement and an effective district attorney's office remain committed to protecting the city's citizens and further reducing crime.

EDUCATING LOUISIANA

Education is another prime concern for the people of Louisiana. Today more than 750,000 young people attend prekindergarten through grade twelve in Louisiana schools. According to the National Education Association, Louisiana ranks forty-third in the nation for public-school teachers' salaries. The average teacher's salary in Louisiana is $8,426 less that the national average. Louisiana ranks thirty-sixth in the amount of money it spends to educate each pupil; the state spends just 3 percent of its gross

Louisiana's Department of Education strives for "a quality public education system of such excellence that all children are given the opportunity to develop to their fullest potential."

LOUISIANA BY PARISH

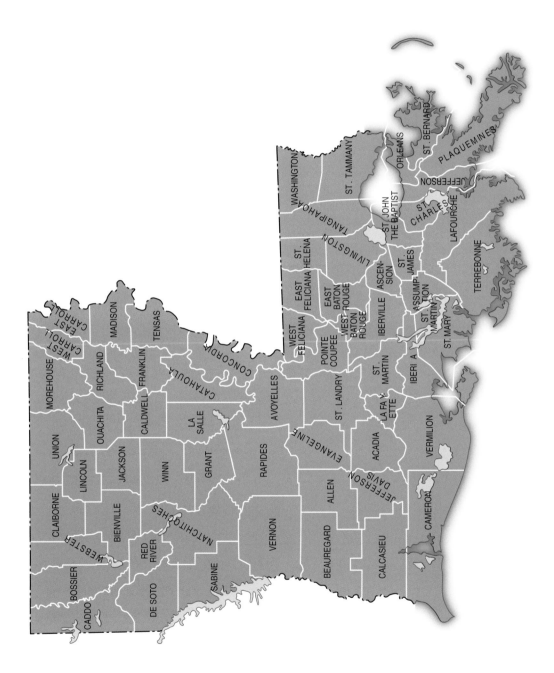

state product on education, which is the fifth lowest amount in the country. According to the American Society of Civil Engineers, Louisiana's schools are in terrible disrepair: 39 percent require extensive repairs and 66 percent are in poor environmental condition.

FOSTERING A HEALTHIER LOUISIANA

Although government spending for health care and human services, including welfare payments to the unemployed, accounts for about 30 percent of the state's total expenditures, Louisiana still faces enormous health-care challenges. According to statistics collected every year by the United Health Foundation, Louisiana ranked lowest in the nation in terms of the health of its citizens in every year but one. It ranks in the bottom five states on six of eighteen individual measures, including the high prevalence of smoking among adults, the percentage of children living in poverty, the percentage of the population without health insurance, the rate of cancer deaths, the infant mortality rate, and the premature death rate. It also ranks in the bottom ten states on five additional measures. From 2003 to 2004, public health spending declined from $35 to $22 per person. More than 827,000 Louisianans—one in five—have no health insurance.

In 1999 the state joined a national initiative called "Healthy People 2010," which aims to bring private and public health-care facilities and professionals together to attack the serious health

Louisiana's Department of Health and Hospital's mission is to "promote health and to ensure access to medical, preventive, and rehabilitative services" to all Louisianans.

problems facing Louisiana's citizens over the coming decade. The goal is to offer community-based services to help people adopt better habits, such as not smoking, exercising, and controling chronic diseases and conditions, like diabetes, obesity, and high blood pressure.

GUARDING AGAINST TERRORISM AND NATURAL DISASTERS

Since the terrorist attacks on the United States in 2001, protecting its citizens from terrorist threats has become a top priority for Louisiana's legislators and law-enforcement personnel. The state's vast oil and gas reserves and the fact that it is home to two of the nation's largest international ports could make the state a prime target for terrorists wishing to disrupt the state and national economies. Funds from the federal government and from the state's own coffers have been used to examine the state's security needs and to develop appropriate response mechanisms to emergencies of all kinds.

In December 2004, Louisiana's U.S. senator Mary Landrieu announced that Louisiana would receive nearly $43 million from the federal government to fund programs designed to prevent, respond to, and recover from terrorist attacks as well as others disasters. "Louisiana's rich energy resources, transportation infrastructure, and defense industry provide a vital backbone to our nation's national security and economy," Senator Landrieu said. "These grants are an important step toward providing our state and local leaders with the tools they need to protect our state from terrorism and care for our citizens if tragedy strikes."

Although guarding against terrorism remains a priority, the state's vulnerability to natural disasters became all too clear after hurricanes Katrina and Rita decimated much of southern Louisiana in 2005. State officials are currently working with federal agencies to better protect Louisiana from hurricanes in the future.

During the 2002 Super Bowl in New Orleans, Louisiana's Air National Guard troops patrolled the Superdome to ensure safety.

CREATING OPPORTUNITY

In order to better promote the health, welfare, and prosperity of the state, the government of Louisiana and its citizens must work together, especially to meet the challenges posed by Hurricane Katrina. Louisiana's rich natural resources, strategic position on the Mississippi River and the Gulf of Mexico, and the creativity and resiliency of its people provide hope for a strong and prosperous economy.

Chapter Five

Facing Great Challenges

The "Big Easy"—that's one of Louisiana's well-deserved nicknames. Both the weather and the people are warm, and it's easy to imagine whiling away lazy hours sitting alongside a meandering bayou or chatting with friends in a New Orleans cafe.

Living in Louisiana is not always so easy, however. According to data collected in 2003 by the U.S. Census Bureau, a greater percentage of people live in poverty here than anywhere else in the nation. More than 20 percent of Louisiana's population lives below the poverty line, compared with about 12 percent of the population nationwide. As of November 2004 the unemployment rate for Louisiana was 5.7 percent, higher than at least thirty-eight other states in the country. Statistics following Hurricane Katrina are unknown.

In December 2004 government officials and experts met at the "Solutions to Poverty" summit, held to focus attention on the economic challenges facing Louisiana. The statistics were grim: even since the 2000 Census, poverty has increased. According to the U.S. Census Bureau American Community Survey, more than 42,000 people joined the ranks of the poor in 2003 alone. More than one in four Louisiana children now live in poverty.

Chili pepper pickers harvest the red-hot peppers the Mclhenny Company of Avery Island grows exclusively for its Tabasco sauce.

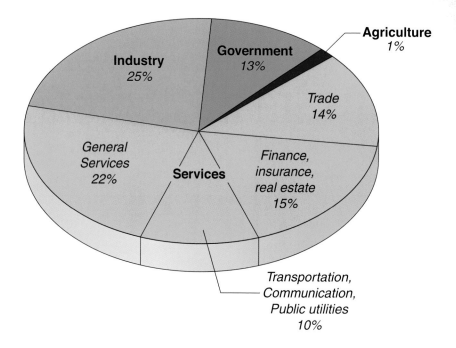

2002 GROSS STATE PRODUCT: $132 Million

- Industry 25%
- Government 13%
- Agriculture 1%
- Trade 14%
- General Services 22%
- Services
- Finance, insurance, real estate 15%
- Transportation, Communication, Public utilities 10%

In East Carroll, a Mississippi River Delta parish in northeastern Louisiana, the percentage has risen to more than one in two children living in poverty. "While the statistics are bleak, hope is not dead," Governor Kathleen Blanco said on the opening day of the summit. One need only look at the state's remarkable natural resources and opportunities for economic growth to keep that hope alive, even considering the new challenges posed by Hurricane Katrina's aftermath

RICH RESERVES, NATURAL BOUNTY, AND MANUFACTURING

Today, as Louisiana struggles to cope with its mounting economic challenges, its citizens continue to look with pride and optimism at the state's vast natural resources. Indeed, from the oil and natural gas reserves beneath it to the mighty Mississippi River and thriving Gulf Coast that link it to the rest of the nation, Louisiana's natural assets are extensive.

Mining and Refining

Without question, Louisiana's greatest natural resource is its stores of oil and natural gas: petroleum and natural gas mining comprise 95 percent of the state's mining income. The state contains just under 10 percent of all known U.S. oil reserves and is the country's third-largest producer of petroleum. It also produces just over one-quarter of all U.S. supplies of natural gas. Louisiana petroleum refineries produce about 15 billion gallons of gasoline every year, making it the nation's third-largest refiner. In addition to producing gasoline, Louisiana refineries also produce jet fuels, lubricants, and some six hundred other petroleum products.

Almost one hundred miles off the Louisiana coast, this oil rig drills for oil, contributing to the state's economy.

Louisiana ranks second in the nation in the production of petrochemicals. More than one hundred major chemical plants are located in the state, producing a variety of "building block" chemicals, fertilizers, and plastics, plus the raw materials for a wide array of other products. Synthetic rubber was first developed and produced commercially in Louisiana, as were a number of other petroleum-related products.

In addition, Louisiana also mines immense quantities of salt, mostly in the southern part of the state. Archaeologists have found tools dating back to AD 1300 that indicate early inhabitants of Avery Island, located in southern Louisiana, gathered salt at a brine spring. The massive salt dome underlying the island was discovered around the time of the Civil War and served the Confederacy until the original mine was flooded by Union troops. After Reconstruction citizens developed a new mine. Today, the salt mine at Avery Island still produces salt for use on icy roads, in industry, and as food, including the salt used in Avery Island's other famous product, Tabasco sauce.

Chili peppers are salted on Avery Island. They will then be mashed, fermented, and aged for three years.

Another important source of revenue for Louisiana is sulfur. The first sulfur mined in America came from Louisiana, and the state is still a principal producer of the mineral. The sulfur industry's growth in Louisiana began in 1932 when Freeport Sulphur Company acquired the sulfur rights to Lake Grande Ecaille and vicinity in Plaquemines Parish. The site is southwest of the Mississippi River and within four miles of the Gulf of Mexico. Port Sulphur, a small city of about three thousand people, remains a center of sulfur mining in the state.

Agriculture

Farmland occupies about 30 percent of the total area of Louisiana, housing more than 25,000 farms. Louisiana is among the top-ten producers in the nation of its three main crops: sugarcane, cotton, and rice. Louisiana's sugarcane industry employs about 27,000 people in twenty-four parishes. They produce about 16 million tons of cane per year, valued at more than $600 million. Cotton earns the state about $350 million per year. Louisiana is the sole source of the Tabasco pepper, made into the Tabasco sauce prized as a condiment around the world.

Successful cotton harvests continue to significantly contribute to the economy of Louisiana.

Forestry

Louisiana has more than 13.9 million acres of forests, including pine, oak, gum, and cypress. More Louisiana timber grows on private than on public property and thus is subject to fewer usage restrictions. Approximately 1 billion board-feet of timber and 3.6 million cords of pulpwood are cut annually to support a variety of forest-related industries, including paper mills, plywood and particleboard plants, furniture and flooring manufacturers, pulp mills, linerboard and containerboard factories, and paper-bag plants.

The abundance of forests in northern Louisiana allows paper mills, for example, to thrive.

Fishing

Louisiana's commercial fishing industry catches about 25 percent of all the seafood landed in America and holds the record for the largest catch ever landed in a single year, 1.9 billion pounds. The state is the largest producer of shrimp and oysters in the United States. Louisiana

A crawfish harvester shows off his fresh catch.

waters also yield menhaden, crab, butterfish, drum, red snapper, tuna, and tilefish as well as a variety of game fish, including tarpon. The state's freshwater fishery is considered the most diverse in the nation. In addition to fish, Louisiana also produces millions of pounds of crawfish annually.

Manufacturing

Louisiana has a diverse manufacturing sector. Its general manufacturing sector includes maritime, military, barge, and recreational vessel shipbuilding, light truck assembly, aerospace and aviation facilities, automobile equipment manufacturing, food processing, and apparel manufacturing. Among the many thousands of products Louisianans create are business telephone systems, electrical equipment, pharmaceuticals, glass products, automobile batteries, specialized vehicles for traveling over marshes, maritime ranging equipment, playground equipment, mobile homes, and yachts and other ships.

Louisiana shipyards build every kind of seagoing vessel, from giant cryogenic ships—used to transport liquefied natural gas—to some of the largest offshore oil and gas exploration rigs in the world. They also build merchant vessels, Coast Guard cutters, barges, tugs, supply boats, fishing vessels, pleasure craft, and river patrol boats.

Unfortunately, Louisiana has lost 21,000 manufacturing jobs since the year 2000, averaging a loss of about five hundred jobs every month. Louisiana exports only 1.5 percent of America's manufactured products.

CREATING AND SERVING

The largest sector of the state's economy consists of service industries. People who work for banks, hospitals, advertising agencies, law firms, and stores all have jobs in the service industry. So do waiters and other people who work in the tourist industry, which is a vital part of Louisiana's economy.

LOUISIANA WORKFORCE

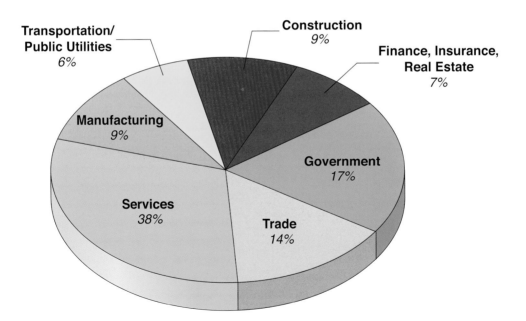

Transportation/
Public Utilities
6%

Construction
9%

Finance, Insurance,
Real Estate
7%

Manufacturing
9%

Government
17%

Services
38%

Trade
14%

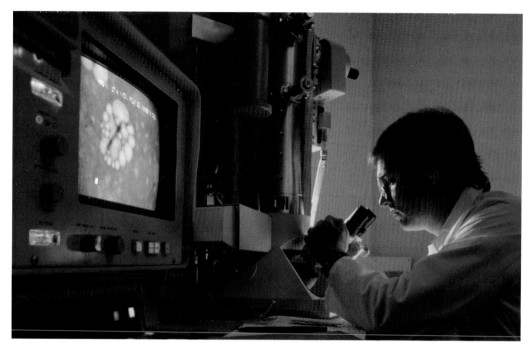

A biotechnology student at the University of Southwest Louisiana examines tiny biological forms.

High Tech and Biotechnology

Several corporations have divisions in Louisiana that employ thousands of people and bring in millions of dollars in revenue. They include Northrop Grumman Corporation and Lockheed Martin.

Biotechnology is the use of biological material in the agricultural industry or in medicine, and Louisiana's universities and private laboratories excel in this area. In fact, scientists at Louisiana State University were the first to bring about the successful birth of a calf from one-quarter of a transplanted embryo. The Pennington Biomedical Research Center is another facility on the cutting edge of this industry. The scientists there study of the role of nutrition in health.

Trade

A young United States purchased Louisiana from the French in 1803 primarily to secure the Mississippi River and the port of New Orleans so that the nation's bounty could be transported throughout the states and around the world. Today, the state remains a major avenue for the import and export of goods. The state's five major ports handle approximately 500 million short tons of cargo a year, including more than 40 percent of all the grain exported by the United States. More than 25 percent of the nation's waterborne exports pass through Louisiana. Its "superport," the Louisiana Offshore Oil Port, is the only facility in the nation able to handle vessels

Dock workers load bags of sugar onto a cargo ship docked in New Orleans, one of the country's busiest ports.

that draw one hundred feet of water, allowing very large oil tankers to reach the state. More than five thousand oceangoing ships call at Louisiana ports each year, along with a seemingly endless stream of barge tows, some of which carry more than 40,000 tons of cargo, more than many seagoing ships.

Thanks to its pivotal location, Louisiana remains a center for foreign investment, with some two hundred foreign companies having almost $16 billion invested in the state, the largest amount of foreign investment in any southeastern state and ninth largest among all states.

Hollywood, Southern Style

Louisiana's film history dates back to a 1908 production of *Faust*, and since then the industry has brought millions of dollars in revenue to the state. Filmmakers have long been entranced by the exotic landscape and architecture, but in recent years, economic factors have attracted them even more. Walt Disney, Warner Bros., Dream Works, and other Hollywood studios have made movies in the state. Recent major motion pictures filmed in Louisiana include *All the King's Men*, starring Sean Penn and Jude Law; *The Dukes of Hazzard*, starring Jessica Simpson and Burt Reynolds; and *Last Holiday*, starring Queen Latifah and LL Cool J. *Ray*, a blockbuster movie about the blues singer Ray Charles, starring Jamie Foxx, was filmed almost entirely in Louisiana.

Tourism

Louisiana tourism is a $9.4-billion industry that employs more than 120,000 people and brings in more than $600 million in state and local taxes each year. There are countless reasons people have visited the Pelican State, including the elegant yet boisterous French Quarter, with its restaurants, bars, galleries, and shops; the deep forests offering plentiful opportunities for hunting, fishing, and camping; and the dozens of cultural festivals held throughout the state. How quickly the tourism sector returns following Hurricane Katrina remains to be seen, but plans are already in the works for Mardi Gras 2006.

EARNING A LIVING

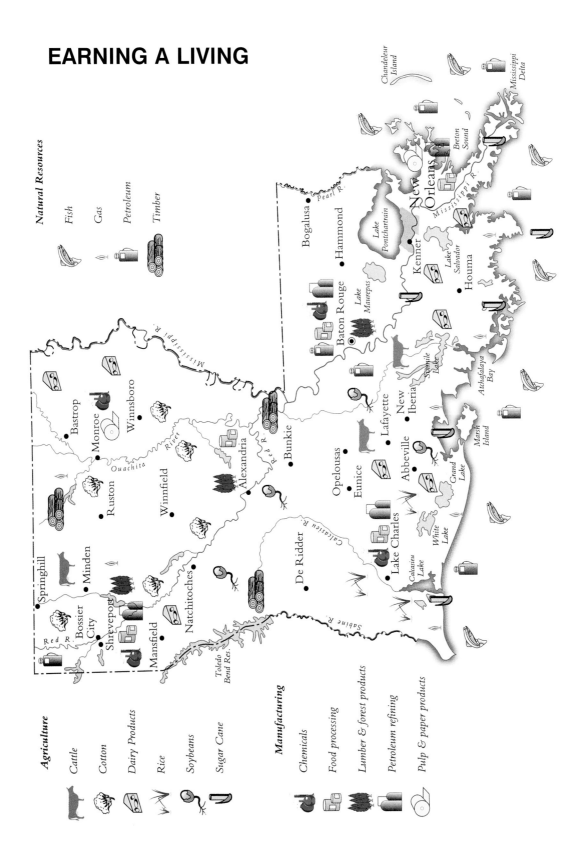

Natural Resources

Fish

Gas

Petroleum

Timber

Agriculture

Cattle

Cotton

Dairy Products

Rice

Soybeans

Sugar Cane

Manufacturing

Chemicals

Food processing

Lumber & forest products

Petroleum refining

Pulp & paper products

Chandeleur Island

Mississippi Delta

Breton Sound

New Orleans

Mississippi R.

Pearl R.

Bogalusa

Hammond

Kenner

Lake Pontchartrain

Lake Salvador

Houma

Lake Maurepas

Baton Rouge

Sixmile Lake

Atchafalaya Bay

New Iberia

Lafayette

Marsh Island

Grand Lake

Abbeville

Opelousas

Eunice

White Lake

Lake Charles

Calcasieu Lake

Mississippi R.

Winnsboro

Bastrop

Monroe

Ouachita River

Ruston

Winnfield

Alexandria

Red R.

Bunkie

Calcasieu R.

De Ridder

Springhill

Minden

Natchitoches

Bossier City

Shreveport

Mansfield

Red R.

Sabine R.

Toledo Bend Res.

The 2005 New Orleans Jazz and Heritage Festival attracted thousands with its food, crafts, and great music.

During the last week in April and the first week in May, millions of music lovers from all over the world come to Louisiana for the New Orleans Jazz and Heritage Festival. More than four thousand musicians, chefs, and craftspeople welcome more than 400,000 music lovers every year. The ten-day festival includes daily concerts performed by the best jazz, gospel, rhythm and blues, and zydeco musicians in the world. Most concerts take place at the Fair Grounds Race Course, which offers more than a dozen sound stages. At night performers entertain in clubs around the city. Every year Jazz Fest earns the city and state about $350 million in revenue, an amount state officials hope will be retained in the years to come.

In December 2004 the state held its first annual Cultural Economy Initiative and Summit, a forum for business and government leaders to discuss ideas for bringing more tourists—and more tourist dollars—into the state by promoting its museums, galleries, and music showcases. "We gather today to reassert and claim ownership of Louisiana as the cultural capital of the South, to declare that Louisiana is the music capital of the world," Lieutenant Governor Mitch Landrieu told attendees. "When we promote economic growth and development—every voice that speaks of tourism, health care, aerospace, military, and medical research . . . will now also speak of the business of culture and recognize that the cultural economy is at the table of economic development as a full partner in making Louisiana a great place to live, work and play."

While almost everyone is aware of Louisiana's traditional role as the Sportsman's Paradise, few realize the real impact that outdoor sports have on the economy. In a 2004 interview with a local reporter, Dwight Landreneau, secretary of Louisiana's Department of Wildlife and Fisheries, pointed out that hunting and fishing totaled "over a billion dollars in economic impact [in 2003]."

Concentrating on increasing tourist dollars, encouraging the growth of the manufacturing sector, especially in the high-tech arena, and protecting the environment so that the state's fishing industry can continue to thrive remain priorities for the government and the people of Louisiana.

CELEBRATING NATURE'S BOUNTY

From Louisiana's rich farmland and waters come many delicious foodstuffs, and Louisianans take every opportunity to celebrate this bounty during fairs and festivals across the state.

Louisiana produces more than 90 percent of all the crawfish in the country, a fact that Breaux Bridge—the "Crawfish Capital of the World"—applauds with gusto every May during the Breaux Bridge Crawfish Festival. Crowley, the center of the state's rice-growing district, throws an International Rice Festival, complete with the coronation of a queen, who flings bags of rice from a colorful float during the annual parade.

In March the town of Amite throws a festival for the oyster, that delectable bivalve southerners love to fry and put into sandwiches called po'boys or eat raw on the half shell with hot sauce. Gonzales, a town located in the heart of Cajun country and the self-proclaimed "Jambalaya Capital of the World," serves thousands of people hearty helpings of the spicy sausage, fish, and rice stew during the Jambalaya Festival.

Strawberries, blueberries, peaches, corn, catfish, crabs, gumbo—Louisiana honors them all with parades, cook-offs, and other festivities that encourage tourists as well as residents to enjoy the bounty.

Chapter Six

Exploring Louisiana

Many people assume that Louisiana has only two landscapes: a hilly, pine-tree–covered north and a swampy, humid south. In truth, the north has its share of swampland and alligators; the south has lush farmland and rolling hills; and nearly every city, town, and bayou village in the state has something special to offer.

People from all over the world visit Louisiana. Many arrive by plane at the Louis Armstrong New Orleans International Airport, named for one of the state's most beloved sons.

THE BIG EASY

Until Hurricane Katrina changed the landscape, the eleven-mile ride from the airport to downtown New Orleans provided a fascinating overview of what life in Louisiana was like today. Just seventy years ago Louisiana had only three thousand miles of paved roads. Fifty-five thousand miles of roads and highways now cover the state.

On the way you'll see typical urban sprawl: small businesses, stores, and factories line the highway, and cars speed by on the route that also leads to and from the state capital of Baton Rouge. Soon, the gleaming skyscrapers of New Orleans come into view.

Louisiana's sights and sounds are unique to this lively state.

The lights of New Orleans reflect in the waters of the Mississippi River at dusk.

"I love coming home to Louisiana and driving into New Orleans," says Joe Peters, a physician who lives in a suburb of the state's largest city. "Right beside the highway, in front of the factories and stores, is the Atchafalaya Swamp, looking as muddy and mysterious as anything." Throughout the state you'll notice that modern industry sits alongside both rugged nature and historic elegance. Cypress trees and dark green waters that hide what lurks beneath let you know you've arrived in Louisiana.

The French Quarter

Once you've arrived in New Orleans, your adventure really begins. You're enveloped at once by new sights, sounds, and aromas. The novelist Anne

Rice describes what makes her hometown so special: "It's the color of the sky—the color of the banana trees—the flowers—the heart. It's walking, breathing, being here."

The city's oldest section is filled with fine examples of eighteenth- and nineteenth-century Creole architecture. Called the French Quarter or the Vieux Carré (Old Square), its narrow streets are lined with picturesque homes, hotels, shops, and restaurants. Residents adorn the railings of their cast-iron balconies with flowers and gather around fountains bubbling in hidden courtyards.

Decorative metal grillwork and blooming flowers adorn this Bourbon Street balcony.

MARDI GRAS: LET THE GOOD TIMES ROLL

For about two weeks starting in January, the city of New Orleans hosts the largest Mardi Gras festival in North America. Marked by a series of elaborate parades, wild parties, elegant balls, and merry-making of all kinds, Mardi Gras in New Orleans has been described as "The Greatest Free Show on Earth."

All of Louisiana's distinct cultures—Native American, African American, Cajun, and others—participate in the festivities. The festival developed out of Catholic traditions. Mardi Gras means "Fat Tuesday" in French, so named because it is the Tuesday before Lent, a time of fasting. Revelers in masks and costumes watch parades of decorated floats wind through the streets. They run to catch fake gold coins, beads, and other trinkets thrown by fully costumed members of krewes (secret organizations), who sponsor the parades.

"Mardi Gras is one big party," one resident of the Big Easy remarks, "and the whole world is invited."

Bourbon Street is the most famous roadway in the Quarter, and it's usually jammed with people enjoying its sights and sounds. Jazz, rhythm and blues, and rock 'n' roll musicians perform both inside the Quarter's many clubs and outside on its sidewalks. Preservation Hall is perhaps the most famous jazz club in the city.

The center of the French Quarter is Jackson Square. The focal point of the original city, Jackson Square contains several historic buildings. Saint Louis Cathedral, one of the oldest cathedrals in the United States, dominates the square with its majestic spires. The Cabildo, now housing a branch of the Louisiana State Museum, was the seat of the Spanish government in the early eighteenth century. In the square itself fortune-tellers read tarot cards, artists paint portraits, and musicians play the blues. One of the best ways to

Originally known as Plaza d'Armas, Jackson Square is a large open area used for parades, concerts, and picnics.

enjoy New Orleans is to stroll through this open-air arena. "This is the first place I come when I visit this city," a tourist from Illinois remarks. "It takes the Midwest right out of me."

On the other side of Jackson Square lies the Mississippi River. Huge oil tankers and other commercial vessels ply these waters, as do tourist steamboats and pleasure craft. The sight of the "Big Muddy"—so named because of its brown color, caused by the tons of sediment it carries—is awesome.

With all of its attractions, many visitors never leave the French Quarter. But New Orleans has much more to offer. The busy commercial Canal Street marks the division between the French Quarter and "Uptown." The first Anglo-Saxon plantation owners developed this part of the city in the early nineteenth century.

Uptown on the Trolley

To visit Uptown, a mixed residential and commercial area, visitors can take a charming streetcar that travels from Canal Street along St. Charles Avenue. The trolley passes through the Garden District, a residential area of antebellum mansions and landscaped gardens. Magazine Street forms the lower border of the Garden District and is a treasure trove of bargain antique shops and boutiques.

Farther uptown, two of the city's major universities—Loyola and Tulane—face tree-lined St. Charles Avenue. You'll find Audubon Park and Audubon Zoo and Gardens just across the street from the universities. A Louisiana swamp exhibit features not only alligators and other creatures of the marsh, but also Cajun architecture and food. Rhinos, black bears, cheetahs, and white tigers are just a few of the zoo residents.

The zoo offers a special tour for those interested in experiencing even more wildlife: visitors can opt to take a riverboat ride from the Uptown zoo back down to the French Quarter where the Aquarium of the Americas sits alongside the river. After a tour of the aquarium and its more than ten thousand swimming residents, visitors can treat themselves to a meal in one of the Quarter's many restaurants.

DOWN ON THE BAYOU IN CAJUN COUNTRY

The Audubon Zoo may give a glimpse of Louisiana wildlife, but the real thing can be seen just a few miles away in Cajun Country. Visitors can take one of the many "swamp tours," and see snowy egrets, blue herons, alligators, and turtles in their natural habitats.

Alligators are a common sight in the swamps of Cajun Country.

But Cajun Country has more than natural beauty. It consists of twenty-two parishes, each one made up of tiny towns, thriving cities, and distinct communities. The commercial center of Cajun Country is Lafayette, the fourth-largest city in the state. About 110,000 people call Lafayette home. Many of them work in the petrochemical industries. The University of Louisiana at Lafayette is located here, along with several fine museums that highlight Cajun history and culture. The Acadian Village depicts early nineteenth-century Cajun life, and the Jean Lafitte Acadian Cultural Center offers exhibits detailing various aspects of Cajun culture.

If Lafayette is the commercial center of Cajun Country, its spiritual heart is the Bayou Teche. This snakelike body of water meanders through a number of historic towns, each with its own square, Catholic church,

Visitors can step back in time to the early nineteenth century and experience the lifestyle of Louisiana's Cajun settlers.

and cemetery. (All of the cemeteries in southern Louisiana are aboveground; the water level in the area is so high that the caskets would float away during heavy rainfall if they were belowground.)

St. Martinville, founded in 1760, was one of the villages in which Acadians settled when they came to Louisiana. At St. Martinville along Bayou Teche is the 157-acre Longfellow-Evangeline State Historic Site, a park where Cajun Creole plantation life of the mid-nineteenth century is recreated.

South of Lafayette is another bayou that runs south all the way to the Gulf of Mexico. Called Bayou Lafourche and nicknamed "the Longest Main Street in America," it flows for ninety miles through some of the world's richest stores of sugarcane, shrimp, oysters, and oil. In this part of the state, it's likely that you'll hear more French than English spoken. Colly Charpentier, former editor of the Thibodaux *Daily Comet*, remembers a store owner saying to a tourist in the town of Lafourche, "You aren't from around here. You must be American." After being damaged by Hurricane Rita in September 2005, Louisiana's southwestern parishes are working hard to restore their communities.

Cajun Country stretches east to west from Lafourche Parish to the Texas border and south to north from the Gulf of Mexico to Avoyelles Parish. You could spend several weeks exploring just this part of the state. If you do, though, you'll miss the other unique attractions Louisiana has to offer, including a glimpse into the antebellum (pre–Civil War) South found in Plantation Country.

PLANTATION COUNTRY

Plantation Country is located in the southeastern part of the state. Flowing through its center is the Mississippi River, whose gift of rich delta soil helped this region to flourish.

PLACES TO SEE

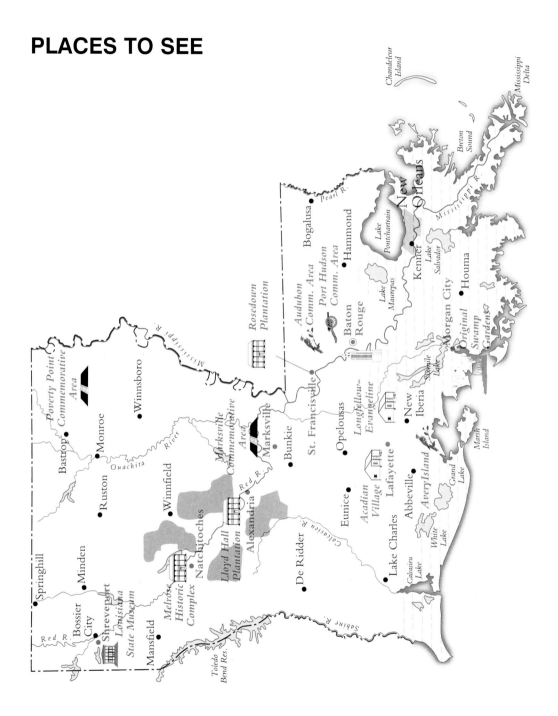

THE EVANGELINE OAK

Alongside the Bayou Teche in one of the oldest towns in Louisiana, St. Martinville, stands the Evangeline Oak. Made famous by Henry Wadsworth Longfellow in his poem *Evangeline: A Tale of Acadie*, this massive tree is a symbol of the Acadian heritage in the United States. In the poem a young Acadian woman named Evangeline waits under the tree in vain for her lover, who has married another and will never return. Evangeline's story symbolizes the patience and loyalty of the Acadian spirit.

Baton Rouge, which became the permanent state capital in 1882, is the economic and cultural center of Plantation Country. Thousands of government workers live in Baton Rouge and its suburbs. Many come to work in the state capitol, the tallest in the country, built by Governor Huey Long. "I can't tell you how many people come in here asking to see the spot where Governor Long was shot," remarks a tour guide. "It is pretty exciting when you think about it."

The view from the capitol's observation deck is extraordinary. You can see huge tankers and other commercial vessels chugging along the

Mississippi River, living proof that Baton Rouge is the nation's ninth-largest port. If you look carefully, you might be able to locate the two-thousand-acre campus of Louisiana State University. More than 30,000 undergraduate and graduate students study in Baton Rouge, and several thousand more study at university branches in Alexandria, New Orleans, and Shreveport.

Your view from above Baton Rouge will no doubt inspire you to explore the lush countryside that surrounds the capital city. To the east lie the Florida parishes, filled with antebellum homes and working farms. In the center of the region, you'll find St. Francisville, an old and charming town.

Pioneer sculptures stand before the state capitol building in Baton Rouge.

To the south and west of Baton Rouge lies the River Road. Lined with elegant plantation homes on one side and oil and gas rigs on the other, the River Road runs south from Baton Rouge almost to New Orleans. On the way you may want to stop and visit Destrehan Plantation, the oldest documented plantation house in the lower Mississippi Valley.

By the time you finish your tour of Plantation Country, you might be ready for a more rugged landscape. For that you can travel north of Baton Rouge into a region called the Crossroads.

Three-hundred-year-old trees cover the entrance leading to Louisiana's Oak Alley plantation.

THE CROSSROADS

Nowhere is the variety of Louisiana's landscape more evident than in the central part of the state. Here you'll find hills and prairies, bayous and rich delta, tiny villages and bustling cities.

At the geographic center of Louisiana lies the city of Alexandria. Located on the banks of the Red River, Alexandria is a commercial and shipping center with a population of more than 45,000. Until 1992 it was the site of England Air Force Base. When the federal government closed that facility, local and state officials and private business owners decided to

TEN LARGEST CITIES

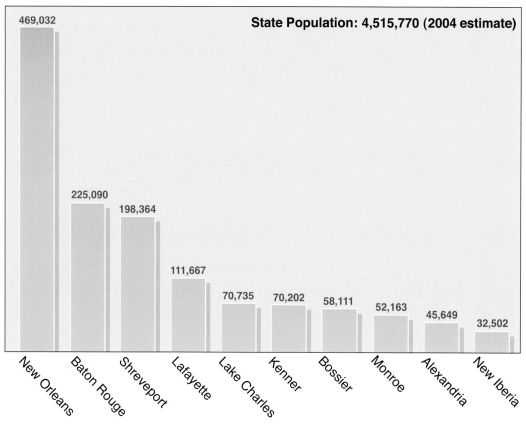

State Population: 4,515,770 (2004 estimate)

City	Population
New Orleans	469,032
Baton Rouge	225,090
Shreveport	198,364
Lafayette	111,667
Lake Charles	70,735
Kenner	70,202
Bossier	58,111
Monroe	52,163
Alexandria	45,649
New Iberia	32,502

transform the base into the England Industrial Airpark and Community, which contains about fifty businesses, three hundred homes, and the Alexandria International Airport.

Lumber and paper products from surrounding areas come to Alexandria for shipment to New Orleans and elsewhere. As you travel around the Crossroads, you'll see some of the pine, oak, and cypress forests upon which Louisiana's forestry industry is built. Farmers also grow cotton, sugarcane, and other crops in the lush farmland of the Red River Delta.

Winn Parish, located deep in the piney hills northwest of Alexandria, is famous for producing three Louisiana governors: Huey Long, his brother Earl, and O.K. Allen. Farther west lies the community of Natchitoches, the very first settlement in Louisiana, which has developed into a modern community of about 18,000 people. The Kisatchie National Forest, a six-thousand-acre forest of hardwood and cypress trees, begins here in the Crossroads and stretches into the northern part of the state. Near Alexandria, the thirty-one-mile Wild Azalea National Recreation Trail offers extravagant floral displays in summer and fall. You can take a canoe ride through the six-mile-long Kisatchie Bayou or hike through the Kisatchie Hills Wilderness Area. Also known as "Louisiana's Little Grand Canyon," this is an area of mesas, cliffs, and canyons.

A fisherman casts a line in Kincaid Lake in Kisatchie National Forest.

Visitors who have made it this far have left the Crossroads and entered Sportsman's Paradise.

SPORTSMAN'S PARADISE

Although this part of Louisiana has its share of bayous and plantation homes, Sportsman's Paradise feels more like the Wild West than the elegant South. This is especially true in the northwestern cities of Shreveport and Bossier City. These twin cities now serve as a center for the sprawling region known as Ark-La-Tex. Ark-La-Tex is a blend of communities in southern Arkansas, northern Louisiana, and eastern Texas. Advertisements for western-style rodeos and Tex-Mex restaurants abound, as do advertisements for Dixieland jazz concerts or Cajun cooking. Horse racing at Louisiana Downs in Bossier City attracts thousands of fans every year.

Traveling east is Webster Parish. The town of Minden offers a glimpse of the German experience in Louisiana at the Germantown Colony Museum. Next is Claiborne Parish, whose courthouse is only one of four pre–Civil War courthouses still in use today.

No tour of Louisiana would be complete without a visit to the twin cities of Monroe and West Monroe. Located on the banks of the scenic Ouachita River, they have a combined population of more than 66,000, many of whom work in the manufacturing and retail trades. The cities have much to offer in the way of arts and culture, including the Strauss Playhouse, an active opera club, and the renowned Masur Museum of Art.

The most direct highway route leads back to New Orleans in about five hours. However, it's unlikely that visitors will be able to resist taking another look at the many geographical and cultural attractions of the Pelican State on the way back down to the Big Easy.

Constructed in 1860, the Claiborne Parish Courthouse was used as the departure point for Confederate troops during the Civil War.

THE FLAG: The state flag was adopted in 1912 and shows a pelican, the state bird, feeding its young in a nest. Beneath the seal is a white ribbon with the words of the state motto. The background is solid blue.

THE SEAL: Adopted in 1902, the state seal shows a pelican at the center, tearing flesh from her own breast to feed her young in the nest — a symbol of Louisiana's caring for its people. The state motto encircles the birds, and the words State of Louisiana surround the circle.

State Survey

Statehood: April 30, 1812

Origin of Name: Louisiana was named in 1682 for the French king Louis XIV by the explorer René-Robert Cavelier, Sieur de La Salle, when he claimed the region for France

Nicknames: Pelican State, Bayou State, Creole State, the Big Easy

Capital: Baton Rouge

Motto: Union, Justice, and Confidence

Animal: Catahoula leopard dog

Bird: Brown pelican

Flower: Magnolia

Tree: Bald cypress

Gem: Agate

Insect: Honeybee

Crustacean: Crawfish

Fossil: Petrified palmwood

Brown pelican

Magnolia blossom

GIVE ME LOUISIANA

In 1970 the State Legislature adopted "Give Me Louisiana" as the official state song in place of an earlier composition entitled "Song of Louisiana." Then in 1977 yet another song was given official status as an equal partner to "Give Me Louisiana": "You Are My Sunshine," written by ex-Governor Jimmie Davis.

Words and Music by Doralice Fontane

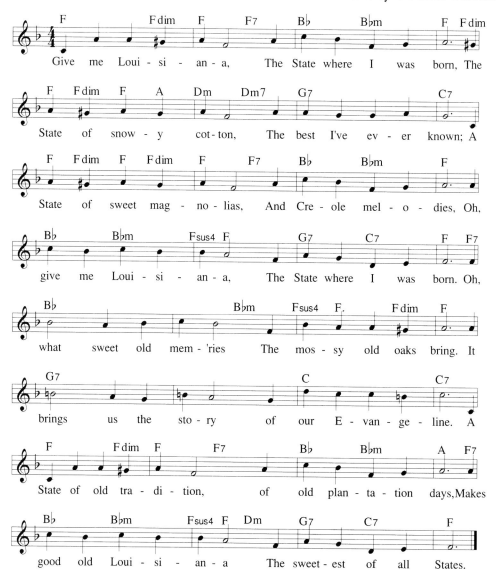

GEOGRAPHY

Highest Point: 535 feet above sea level, at Driskill Mountain

Lowest Point: 5 feet below sea level, at New Orleans

Area: 51,843 square miles

Greatest Distance, North to South: 283 miles

Greatest Distance, East to West: 315 miles

Bordering States: Arkansas to the north, Mississippi to the east, Texas to the west; the Gulf of Mexico lies to the south

Hottest Recorded Temperature: 114 degrees Fahrenheit at Plain Dealing on August 10, 1936

Coldest Recorded Temperature: −16 degrees Fahrenheit at Minden on February 13, 1899

Average Annual Precipitation: 56 inches

Major Rivers: Atchafalaya, Black, Calcasieu, Mississippi, Ouachita, Pearl, Red

Major Lakes: Bistineau, Black, Borgne, Caddo, Calcasieu, Grand, Maurepas, Pontchartrain, Sabine, Salvador, White

Trees: bald cypress, beech, black walnut, hickory, longleaf pine, magnolia, overcup oak, pawpaw, sassafras, shortleaf pine, sweet gum, tupelo

Wild Plants: azalea, camellia, golden club, hibiscus, honeysuckle, iris, jasmine, lily, lotus, marsh hay, milkweed, orchid, pickerelweed, Spanish moss, wild rice

Animals: alligator, beaver, black bear, bobcat, dolphin, diamondback terrapin, Florida panther, gray fox, gray wolf, green water snake, manatee, mink, muskrat, nutria, opossum, raccoon, river otter, sea turtle, skunk, squirrel, sperm whale, weasel, white-tailed deer, wild hog

Manatee

Birds: bald eagle, brown pelican, dove, egret, goose, gull, heron, mallard duck, Mississippi kite, peregrine falcon, pintail duck, quail, red-cockaded woodpecker, teal duck, tern, whooping crane, wild turkey, woodcock

Fish: bass, bluefish, bream, catfish, crappie, crawfish, flounder, grouper, oyster, perch, pompano, redfish, shrimp, Spanish mackerel, sturgeon

Endangered Animals: bald eagle, black bear, brown pelican, green sea turtle, interior least tern, loggerhead sea turtle, pallid sturgeon, red-cockaded woodpecker, red wolf, pink mucket, hawksbill sea turtle, Kemp's ridely sea turtle, leatherback sea turtle, finback whale, humpback whale

Endangered Plants: Louisiana quillwort, American chaffseed

Egret

TIMELINE

c. 2000 BC The first natives populate Louisiana.

c. 1800–700 BC The people of Poverty Point, in what is today northeastern Louisiana, establish a highly developed culture.

c. 300 BC Native Americans live in northeastern Louisiana and build huge burial mounds.

AD 500 Caddos build large villages and ceremonial centers with temple mounds in northern Louisiana.

1541 Hernando de Soto discovers the Mississippi River.

1682 René-Robert Cavelier, Sieur de La Salle, claims the region watered by the Mississippi for France.

1699 Louisiana becomes a royal French colony.

1714 Natchitoches, first permanent settlement, is founded.

1718 New Orleans founded and named for Philippe, duc d'Orléans.

1719 First large-scale importation of African slaves.

1751 Jesuit priests introduce sugarcane.

1762 France cedes Louisiana west of the Mississippi to Spain.

1763 France cedes Louisiana east of the Mississippi to England.

1764 Acadians begin arriving from Canada.

1775–1783 American Revolution.

1788 and 1794 Much of New Orleans is destroyed by fire.

1800 Spain cedes Louisiana west of the Mississippi back to France.

1803 United States purchases Louisiana from France.

1812 Louisiana admitted to the Union as the eighteenth state.

1812–1815 War of 1812 between the United States and Great Britain.

1815 British are defeated in the Battle of New Orleans.

1838 First official Mardi Gras celebration in New Orleans.

1861 Louisiana secedes from the Union; joins the Confederate States of America.

1861–1865 United States Civil War.

1862 Federal troops capture New Orleans.

1877 Louisiana readmitted to the Union.

1901 Oil discovered in Jefferson Davis Parish.

1915 New Orleans music first called "jazz."

1926 Waterways connecting Lake Charles to the Gulf of Mexico open.

1928–1932 Huey P. Long Jr. serves as governor of Louisiana; elected to U.S. Senate in 1930.

1935 Former governor Huey Long assassinated in Baton Rouge.

1948–1952 Earl K. Long serves as governor.

1947 First offshore oil well drilled.

1956 World's longest overwater highway bridge, the Causeway, opens, crossing Lake Pontchartrain.

1960 Public-school integration begins in New Orleans.

1977 Ernest Morial elected as New Orleans's first black mayor.

1984 New Orleans hosts Louisiana World Exposition.

1991 Edwin Edwards beats David Duke in gubernatorial election.

1992 Hurricane Andrew causes extensive damage to southern Louisiana.

1994 New Orleans International Airport expands, making it an important transportation hub for the state and region.

2001 The terrorist bombings of the World Trade Center and the Pentagon send shock waves throughout the state and the nation; Louisiana focuses more of its resources on public safety.

2005 Two mammoth hurricanes, Katrina and Rita, devastate much of southern Louisiana, forever changing the state's landscape, economy, and even population make-up and distribution.

ECONOMY

Agricultural Products: Soybeans, cotton, rice, sugarcane, corn, yams, sorghum, pecans, beef and dairy cattle, hogs, chickens, shrimp, crawfish, catfish

Manufactured Products: Petrochemicals, chemicals, transportation equipment, paper products, processed foods, building materials, electrical equipment, metal products, lumber, printed materials, shipbuilding

Business and Trade: Wholesale and retail sales, finance, insurance, real estate, banking, research, tourism, commercial fishing, shipping, transportation

CALENDAR OF CELEBRATIONS

Mardi Gras Beginning in January, New Orleans celebrates this carnival with food and fun for weeks before the forty days of Lent begin on Ash Wednesday, the day after "Fat Tuesday," *Mardi Gras* in French. Extravagant parades feature floats, marching bands, and masqueraders in flamboyant costumes. Balls are held throughout the city.

Festival International de Louisiane In mid-April, Lafayette is host to hundreds of artists from around the world who gather to celebrate the performing and visual arts.

Baton Rouge Blues Week Baton Rouge honors Louisiana's musical heritage for a week in April with a festival of blues, Cajun, zydeco, and gospel music.

Breaux Bridge Crawfish Festival On the first weekend in May, Breaux Bridge celebrates its fame as "Crawfish Capital of the World" with one of Louisiana's largest festivals. Cajun food, dances, music, folklore, crafts, and contests, including a crawfish race, draw thousands each year.

Contraband Days For two weeks in early May, Lake Charles celebrates the role of the pirate Jean Lafitte in Louisiana's history. Festivities include boat races, concerts, arts and crafts, and midway entertainment.

"Le Cajun" Music Awards Ceremony and Festival Held in August in Lafayette, the festival features Cajun music, crafts, and food, and culminates in the Cajun French Music Association's "Le Cajun" Music Awards.

Louisiana Shrimp and Petroleum Festival Every Labor Day weekend, Morgan City hosts Louisiana's oldest chartered harvest celebration. Festivities include a parade, music, amusement rides, a hands-on children's village, storytelling, and fireworks. A special feature is the blessing of the shrimp boats and the ships that transport Louisiana's oil.

Louisiana Sugar Cane Festival and Fair On the last weekend in September, New Iberia celebrates one of Louisiana's major products with an agricultural show, displays of quilts, parades, and music. A sugar cookery competition is featured, as well as a coronation and ball.

Festivals Acadiens The largest Cajun festival in the world takes place every September in Lafayette. The festival celebrates all things Cajun, including food, music, crafts, and history.

State Fair of Louisiana Shreveport is home to the state fair, one of the largest fairs in the country. The October fair features amusements, food, music, agricultural exhibits, and livestock competitions.

Natchitoches Festival of Lights Louisiana's oldest permanent settlement welcomes the Christmas season on a Saturday in late November with a brilliant festival of lights. Some 300,000 lights are turned on and displayed throughout the city for the entire season.

STATE STARS

Louis "Satchmo" Armstrong (1900?–1971), trumpeter and singer, was born in New Orleans. He first played the coronet at a boys' home and then with King Oliver's Creole Jazz Band in Chicago. Armstrong developed a distinctive singing and playing style that made him a headliner on tours around the world and earned him the nickname "Satchmo," for his satchel-sized mouth. Armstrong is considered to be one of the all-time greatest jazz musicians.

Louis Armstrong

Truman Capote (1924–1984), born in New Orleans, gave up formal schooling at the age of seventeen and settled in New York City to begin his writing career. His first novel, *Other Voices, Other Rooms*, appeared in 1948 and made him an instant success. Capote continued his career, publishing short stories and novels, including *The Grass Harp* and *Breakfast at Tiffany's*. In 1966 Capote was applauded for his book *In Cold Blood*, in which he combined his talents as a novelist and as a reporter to tell the story of a mass murder in Kansas. Many of Capote's works were adapted for films, television, and the stage.

Marie Therese Coincoin (1742–1816?) was born as a slave, probably near Natchitoches. As a young woman she lived with a French planter who in 1778 bought her freedom and eventually gave her a large amount of land. Coincoin worked the land herself and with the help of slaves, cultivating fields of corn, tobacco, and cotton and raising cattle. She trapped bears and exported their grease as far as Europe. With the profits from her land, she bought the freedom of nearly all of her children. After her death the land was divided among them.

Harry Connick Jr. (1967–   ), born in New Orleans, showed exceptional talent at an early age. He played the piano in the annual New Orleans Jazz and Heritage Festival from the time he was eight, and as a teenager played in jazz bands in New Orleans clubs. After moving to New York City, Connick launched a singing career. He was heard on the soundtrack of the film *When Harry Met Sally* in 1989. The recording was one of the few jazz releases to be among the top ten on the pop charts. In 1990 Connick won a Grammy Award for the best male jazz vocal performance.

Antoine "Fats" Domino (1928–), born in New Orleans, learned to play the piano as a child and began playing professionally in 1948. He gained prominence, as well as his nickname, with the 1949 recording "The Fat Man." Domino went on to produce his rhythm and blues sound in the 1950s with such hits as "Ain't That a Shame," "Blueberry Hill," and "I'm Walkin'." Domino's recording career lasted into the early 1970s, when he began touring the nightclub circuit both in the United States and abroad.

Elizabeth Meriwether Gilmer (1861–1951) was born in Tennessee but made New Orleans her home for most of her life. In 1894, under the pen name Dorothy Dix, Gilmer began writing an advice column in the New Orleans newspaper the *Times-Picayune*. She dispensed advice on love, life, and how to cope in her column "Dorothy Dix Talks." It was estimated that she had some 60 million readers around the world.

Elizabeth Meriwether Gilmer

Louis Moreau Gottschalk (1829–1869), pianist and composer, was born in New Orleans. As a prodigy, he studied the piano and violin, and at the age of thirteen toured Europe, giving recitals. In the United States, Gottschalk became one of the most prominent concert performers of his time, playing not only the music of European composers but also his own popular romantic works, including piano pieces, several symphonies, and two operas.

Shirley Ann Grau (1929–   ), a native of New Orleans, is a novelist and short-story writer. She first won acclaim for her book *The Black Prince and Other Stories*, published in 1955. Her first novel, *The Hard Blue Sky*, depicts a community of French-Spanish descendants of early Louisiana pioneers. She went on to write several additional books, including *The House on Coliseum Street*, *The Condor Passes*, and *The Keepers of the House*, which won the 1965 Pulitzer Prize for Fiction.

Lillian Hellman (1907–1984), born in New Orleans, began her writing career as a reporter in New York City in the 1920s. Her first stage success was the 1934 play *The Children's Hour*, which was followed by *Days to Come* and *The Little Foxes*, plus many others. Hellman's plays often reflect her criticism of social and political injustice, such as the anti-Nazi drama *Watch on the Rhine*, which won the Drama Critics Circle Award in 1941. Her autobiographical works include *An Unfinished Woman* and *Pentimento*.

Clementine Hunter (1886–1988), a folk artist, was born on a plantation near Cloutierville. Around the late 1920s Hunter began working as a domestic on the Melrose Plantation near Natchitoches. It was there she developed her artistic talent, painting scenes of everyday life as well as animals and religious themes. Her works were exhibited in the New Orleans Arts and Crafts shows, and she was the first black artist to receive an exhibition at the New Orleans Museum of Art, in 1955. During her long lifetime Hunter's works were shown in galleries around the country, and many are now part of permanent museum collections.

Mahalia Jackson (1912–1972) was born in New Orleans and early on developed a love for blues music. At sixteen Jackson moved to Chicago, Illinois, where she sang in churches and began to make recordings of gospel music. In 1947 Jackson's recording of "Move On Up a Little" became the first million-selling gospel record. Her recordings, live concerts, and television performances earned her the reputation as the world's greatest gospel singer. As an ambassador of music, Jackson

Mahalia Jackson

toured Europe and sang at the White House for President John F. Kennedy, as well as at Martin Luther King Jr.'s March on Washington in 1963. When she died in January 1972, 45,000 people attended her funeral to honor her.

Jean Lafitte (1770s?–1820s?) was born in France, but little is known of his early life there. Around 1810 he was in Louisiana, leading a band of smugglers who operated from the islands in Barataria Bay. Lafitte and his buccaneers sold their smuggled goods and slaves to merchants and planters. Lafitte achieved fame when he aided the American cause in the Battle of New Orleans during the War of 1812. Although pardoned for his former criminal acts, he continued to lead bands of privateers and was famous as a pirate in the Caribbean until he disappeared in about 1825.

Huddie Ledbetter (1888–1949), better known as Leadbelly, was a composer and singer born in Morringsport. Leadbelly was a leading figure in the revival of folk music in America and Europe. He was raised under rough conditions in Texas. He spent many years in prison for murder, attempted murder, and assault. Folklorists John and Alan Lomax discovered him while he was in prison and recorded his music for the Library of Congress in the 1930s. Two of his most popular songs are "On Top of Old Smokey" and "Good Night, Irene."

Jean-Baptiste Le Moyne, Sieur de Bienville (1680–1768), explorer, colonial official, and founder of New Orleans, was born in Montreal, Canada. He explored the Mississippi and Red rivers and helped establish colonies at Biloxi, Mississippi, and on Mobile Bay. While serving as governor of France's Louisiana colony, he selected the site for a new settlement on the east bank of the Mississippi River in 1718 and named it Orleans in honor of France's regent, the duc d'Orléans.

Elmore Leonard (1925–   ), writer of Westerns and mysteries, was born in New Orleans. He wrote short stories, novels, and screenplays for many years until he achieved fame with his suspense stories. Leonard's books are not just thrillers but realistic crime novels with believable characters, many of them living on the fringes of society. His first novel, *The Big Bounce*, published in 1969, was followed by works that include *Stick*, *Glitz*, *Get Shorty*, and *Pronto*.

Huey Pierce Long Jr. (1893–1935), governor of Louisiana and U.S. senator, was born in Winn Parish. Long was a Populist politician who championed the cause of the poor. As governor he promoted social-welfare and public projects while retaining nearly complete control over the state government through patronage. Although he attacked big business for its greed, Long was accused of enriching himself at the public's expense. As a senator his "Share the Wealth" plan made him a national figure. In 1935 Long was preparing to challenge the reelection of President Roosevelt when he was assassinated in the capitol building he had built in Baton Rouge.

Wynton Marsalis (1961–   ), trumpeter, bandleader, and cofounder of New York City's Lincoln Center Jazz Orchestra, was born in New Orleans. Trained in both classical music and jazz, Marsalis has toured the United States and abroad. In 1983 he was the first instrumentalist to win Grammy awards as both a jazz performer and a classical soloist. Marsalis has composed music for films and ballet and has appeared on television as a spokesperson for the rich tradition of jazz.

Wynton Marsalis

Ferdinand "Jelly Roll" Morton (1890–1941), born in New Orleans, was a jazz pianist and composer who began playing the piano in his teens. In 1923 Morton settled in Chicago. Under the name Jelly Roll Morton and His Red Hot Peppers, he recorded his own jazz piano compositions and arrangements. Morton's career as a recording artist was at its height in the 1920s, but his music became less popular in the 1930s, when big bands and swing music became the rage. Morton is considered one of the first great jazz composers, but he did not receive widespread recognition until after his death, when interest in traditional jazz was revived.

Camille Nickerson (1888–1982), born in New Orleans, devoted her life to arranging, collecting, and preserving the Creole music of her ancestors. An accomplished musician, Nickerson also toured widely under the stage name The Louisiana Lady, performing Creole music in concert. She gave up performing in the 1920s to teach at Howard University in Washington, D.C., where she continued to research and promote Creole folk music.

Homer Adolph Plessy (?–1925), the plaintiff in the Supreme Court case *Plessy v. Ferguson* in 1896, is thought to have been born in New Orleans and to have worked as a carpenter. Plessy became famous when, in 1892, he challenged the Jim Crow laws of Louisiana by sitting in the white section of a railroad train. He was removed and taken to jail in New Orleans. Backed by a black citizens' group, Plessy appealed his case to the Supreme Court. The court ruled against Plessy, stating that segregation in public facilities was legal, a decision that was not overturned until 1954.

Paul Prudhomme (1940–   ) was born on a farm near Opelousas in Acadian country. He began cooking with his mother at the age of seven. At seventeen he set out to become a cook, working in restaurants around the country for twelve years to learn culinary techniques. He returned to Louisiana and in 1979 opened K-Paul's Louisiana Kitchen in New Orleans, which

Paul Prudhomme

features traditional Creole and Cajun cooking as well as Prudhomme's unique creations. He is the author of several cookbooks, has been featured on television cooking programs, and in 1980 was the first American chef to receive France's *Mérite Agricole* Award.

Norbert Rillieux (1806–1894) was born in New Orleans. His father was a wealthy plantation owner; his mother was a slave. Educated in Paris as an engineer, Rillieux returned to Louisiana and began working for a sugar refinery. In 1845 he invented a system for refining sugar that greatly reduced the cost of production. Rillieux's system is still used today.

Corinne Boggs "Cokie" Roberts (1943–   ), reporter, news analyst, and commentator, was born in New Orleans. Roberts's journalistic career includes work as a reporter for radio stations in New York City and Los Angeles as well as for CBS News in Athens, Greece. She also served as a correspondent for National Public Radio and was a regular interviewer and commentator on the television program *This Week with David Brinkley*. Roberts has won the Broadcast Award of the National Organization of Working Women and the Broadcast Award of the National Women's Political Caucus.

William "Bill" Russell (1934–   ) was born in Monroe and later moved to Oakland, California. As a college sophomore Russell became one of the best-known basketball players on the West Coast. In 1956 Russell joined the Boston Celtics, where his talents as a defensive player helped the Celtics win the world championship eight years in a row. Before becoming the Celtics's player/coach in 1967, Russell was named the NBA's Most Valuable Player five times. In 1975 Russell was inducted into the Basketball Hall of Fame.

Edward Douglass White (1845–1921), the only Supreme Court justice from Louisiana, was born in Lafourche Parish. White served in the Confederate army during the Civil War and began his political career in Louisiana's state senate. He was later elected to the U.S. Senate, where he staunchly supported states' rights. In 1894 White was appointed associate justice of the Supreme Court, and in 1910 he was appointed chief justice, a position he held until his death. One of White's major contributions while serving on the court was his decision to strike down a discriminatory law that prevented blacks from voting.

TOUR THE STATE

Poverty Point State Historic Site (Pioneer) This prehistoric site is a complex of ancient Indian ceremonial mounds dating from between 1800 and 700 BC. People moved thousands of tons of earth by hand to create the mounds.

Louisiana State Exhibit Museum (Shreveport) Dioramas and murals depict Louisiana's prehistory as well as the state's many resources.

Melrose Historic Complex (Natchitoches) Melrose is the estate first created by Marie Therese Coincoin. There are eight restored buildings, including the Yucca House, whose walls are made of river-bottom mud and Spanish moss, and the main mansion.

Loyd Hall Plantation (Cheneyville) This pre–Civil War estate is the center of a working cotton plantation. Visitors can search for bullet holes and arrowheads and possibly hear ghosts playing violins.

Marksville State Historic Site (Marksville) This area contains the ruins of an Indian settlement, including earthen mounds, dating from AD 1 to 400. Its museum houses Indian artifacts and exhibits describing the culture.

Acadian Village (Lafayette) This replica of a nineteenth-century village features Acadian architecture with homes, a general store, and a chapel. Acadian crafts are also displayed.

Rosedown Plantation State Historic Site (St. Francisville) Rosedown, with its 371 acres of historic gardens and moss-draped oaks, is a pre–Civil War estate on which visitors can view the restored contents of the mansion.

Audubon State Historic Site (St. Francisville) The park features the Oakley Plantation House, where John James Audubon painted most of his *Birds of America* portraits, as well as a bird sanctuary.

Port Hudson State Historic Site (Port Hudson) Included here is part of the battlefield on which the siege of Port Hudson occurred during the Civil War—the first major battle in which African American Union troops participated. Civil War guns, trenches, and battle reenactments are featured.

State Capitol (Baton Rouge) The 450-foot-high capitol was built by Huey Long and was the site of his assassination. Constructed of more than thirty kinds of marble, it is the tallest state capitol building in the United States.

Rivertown (Kenner) A historic district in a Victorian setting, Rivertown features a science center, a wildlife museum, a Mardi Gras museum, a toy train museum, and a children's castle.

Louisiana State Museum (New Orleans) This museum comprises several landmark buildings, including the Cabildo, where the transfer of ownership of Louisiana from France to the United States took place. Exhibits here trace Louisiana's history from exploration through Reconstruction. The Presbytère, built on the site of a home for monks, houses exhibits on Louisiana's cultural history. The Old U.S. Mint, an 1835 landmark building, houses exhibits on jazz and Mardi Gras. The 1850 House, a row house, contains furnishings and artifacts depicting Creole lifestyle in the nineteenth century.

Aquarium of the Americas (New Orleans) With four major aquatic habitats, including a Caribbean reef, the aquarium is home to ten thousand animals and one of the world's largest shark collections.

Audubon Zoo (New Orleans) More than 1,500 animal species are housed in their natural habitats in the zoo, including white alligators in a swamp exhibit.

Musée Conti Historical Wax Museum (New Orleans) Visitors learn the history of New Orleans as they view wax figures that include Napoleon Bonaparte, Jean Lafitte, Andrew Jackson, and Louis Armstrong.

Confederate Museum (New Orleans) Louisiana's oldest museum exhibits uniforms, weapons, paintings, flags, and other artifacts from the Civil War.

Garden District (New Orleans) This district contains elegant mansions built in the 1850s by wealthy businesspeople who did not want to live in the crowded French Quarter.

Grand Isle (an island south of New Orleans) Located at the entrance to Barataria Bay, this fishing village is home to a few descendants of Jean Lafitte's pirate band.

Jungle Gardens (Avery Island) Not really an island, this site covers an old salt mine. The gardens abound with all kinds of tropical flowers. A bird sanctuary draws great flocks of egrets, herons, ducks, and other wild birds.

Original Swamp Gardens (Morgan City) Visitors tour 3.5 acres of swampland depicting the habitat and animals of the Atchafalaya Swamp.

Conrad Rice Mill (New Iberia) Visitors can tour the oldest rice mill in the United States, which includes a replica of the original company store and displays of Cajun crafts and folklore.

Longfellow-Evangeline Historic Site (St. Martinville) Said to be the setting of Longfellow's poem "Evangeline: A Tale of Acadie," this site features the Evangeline Monument as well as the Evangeline Oak, under which visitors can gather to listen to storytellers and musicians. A museum features mementos of the Acadian people who settled here.

FUN FACTS

When Andy Bowen and Jack Burke battled in the boxing ring in New Orleans in April 1893, they made history. Their fight lasted 7 hours, 19 minutes and went 110 rounds. It was the world's longest boxing match, and it ended in a tie.

Although the term "Dixie," used to describe the South, is thought to be derived from the Mason-Dixon Line, it could be from the French word *dix*—meaning "ten," which appeared on Louisiana banknotes.

Chef Paul Prudhomme made blackened redfish so popular that a ban was put on catching and serving the fish. Prudhomme and other chefs had to turn to blackened yellowfin tuna.

Cajun dancing is sometimes called "chank-a-chanking" because of the sound made by the little iron triangle that is part of a traditional Cajun band, along with the fiddle and the accordion.

The first Tarzan movie, released in 1918, was filmed in Louisiana.

To help increase its population in the 1700s, the colony of Louisiana encouraged young women in France to emigrate. The women were recruited from orphanages or from "poor but respectable" families. Called Casket Girls because they brought their belongings in a "casket," or chest, they were watched over by the nuns of the Ursuline Convent in New Orleans. One of the nuns' tasks was to help the girls find husbands.

New Orleans's Metairie Cemetery boasts a 60-foot-high monument to Mary Moriarty. It is said that her husband, an Irish immigrant, built the monument so that the people who had snubbed his wife in life would have to look up to her in death.

Find Out More

There's lots more to learn about Louisiana. If you'd like to explore the Pelican State further, look in your school library, local library, bookstore, or video store. Here are a few titles to ask for.

GENERAL STATE BOOKS

Bjorklund, Ruth and Christopher Santoro. *Louisiana* (It's My State!). New York: Benchmark Books, 2005.

Gildart, Leslie S. *Louisiana: The Pelican State.* Minneapolis: Rebound by Sagebrush, 2003.

Glaser, Jason. *Louisiana*. Mankato, Minnesota: Capstone Press, 2003.

Heinrichs, Ann. *Louisiana*. Minneapolis: Compass Point Books, 2003.

Ladoux, Rita. *Louisiana: Hello U.S.A.* Minneapolis: Lerner Publications, 2001.

Prieto, Anita C. and Laura Knorr. *P is for Pelican: A Louisiana Alphabet*. Chelsea, MI: Sleeping Bear Press, 2004.

Reed, Jennifer. *Louisiana*. Berkeley Heights, NJ: Enslow, 2003.

San Souci, Dan and David Catrow. *Little Pierre: A Cajun Story from Louisiana*. New York: Silver Whistle, 2003.

SPECIAL LOUISIANA INTEREST BOOKS

Aaseng, Nathan. *Plessy v. Ferguson.* Lucent Books, 2003.

Bronston, Barri. *The Lobster Kids' Guide to New Orleans*. Montreal: The Lobster Press, 2002.

Collins, David. *Huey Long: Talker and Doer*. New Orleans: Pelican Publishing Company, 2003.

Foran, Jill. *Mardi Gras*. New York: Weigl Publishers, 2003.

McAuliffe, Emily. *Louisiana Facts and Symbols*. Mankato, Minnesota: Bridgestone Press, 2003.

Pascoe, Elaine. *Into Wild Louisiana: Jeff Corwin Experience*. Blackbirch Press, 2003.

DVDS

Discoveries America: Louisiana. Bennett-Watt Media, 2004.
Louisiana Blues Musical Documentary B. City Hall Records, 2005.

WEB SITES

Welcome to Louisiana
www.louisiana.gov
This Web site offers official information about the state's government agencies and programs, from how a resident obtains a driver's license to the latest in political and economic news.

Louisiana
www.50states.com/louisian.htm
If you want to find out more about Louisiana's symbols, flags, government, and history, visit this site, which is chock-full of links to other useful Web sites.

Louisiana Department of Wildlife and Fisheries

www.wlf.state.la.us

The Louisiana Department of Wildlife and Fisheries offers all you need to know about hunting, fishing, and boating in Louisiana, along with information about the department's extensive educational programs.

Louisiana Department of Environmental Quality

www.deq.state.la.us

This state-sponsored site focuses on issues vital to the environmental health of Louisiana, including recycling, air quality, and water pollution. The Louisiana Department of Environmental Quality Web site also offers extensive educational resources and information.

LaCoast

www.lacoast.gov

Funded by the federal Coastal Wetlands Planning, Protection, and Restoration Act of 1990, this local Web site focuses on the challenges faced by Louisiana to keep its precious wetlands safe and productive. Included on the Web site is access to the agency's magazine, *WaterMarks*.

Audubon Nature Institute

www.auduboninstitute.org

This interactive Web site offers visitors a chance to explore the museums and nature trails associated with the Audubon Institute, including the Louisiana Nature Trail, the Audubon Zoo, the Aquarium of the Americas, and the Center for Research of Endangered Species.

Index

Page numbers in **boldface** are illustrations and charts.

ABOUT THE AUTHOR

Suzanne LeVert has written many books for children and young adults on a wide variety of subjects. Ms. Levert lived in New Orleans for seven years, getting to know and love its people and culture as she attended Tulane Law School and then worked as an Assistant District Attorney. She moved to Virginia a month before Hurricane Katrina hit New Orleans. She continues to write and practice law.